Praise for

"There is a moment in the life of every victorious Christian when he is freed from the burden of selfish pursuits by realizing the glory of Christ's Commission. This masterful book is a clear defense of the reasonableness of that moment and is written to create that life-changing moment for you!"

—Aaron B., church planter in North Africa

"Everyone seems to admire missionaries, but there seems to be such mystery about how someone actually becomes one! Jake brings clarity to the issue biblically and practically in such a way that challenges the status quo but also thrills the heart."

—Philip Bassham, church planter in Thailand,
Vision Baptist Missions

"Reading this book just might cause you to rise up and do something with your life. The dam might break, the flood of God's Word just might break loose and flood the parched ground all over the world!"

—Austin Gardner, church-planting pastor,
Vision Baptist Church, Alpharetta, GA
Former church planter in Peru

"As a missionary and as an avid reader of all things 'missions,' I find Jake Taube's *Send Me, I'll Go* insightful and gripping. The fact that these ideas come from a thoughtful young missionary currently on the battlefield makes it a rare gem."

—Chris Gardner, church planter,
Peru Ministry

"Come face-to-face with your inner fears and excuses for not taking the gospel to those who have least heard. This book will call you out and threaten to reshape your paradigm like few have. Every committed Christian must read this game-changer on global missions!"

—Jason Holt, Chile Church Planting

"Jake hits the nail on the head as he investigates this troubling trend and exposes several misconceptions concerning the call of God, the purpose of the church and the Great Commission itself. This is a must-read for anyone who desires to take the next step from understanding the need to making a difference."

—Tyler M., church planter in North Africa

"*Send Me, I'll Go* is the kind of book that will be used to mobilize generations of exported disciple makers—those who will not only surrender their lives to be thrust into the dark places of the world but who are willing to pay whatever cost necessary to make disciples."

—Mark Tolson, church planter,
Project China

SEND ME, I'LL GO

SEND ME, I'LL GO

Letting the Mission Choose Your Direction

Jake Taube

CLC PUBLICATIONS

Fort Washington, PA 19034

Send Me, I'll Go
Published by CLC Publications

U.S.A.
P.O. Box 1449, Fort Washington, PA 19034

UNITED KINGDOM
CLC International (UK)
51 The Dean, Alresford, Hampshire, SO24 9BJ

© 2015 by Jake Taube
All rights reserved. Published 2015

Printed in the United States of America

ISBN (paperback): 978-1-61958-182-1
ISBN (e-book): 978-1-61958-183-8

Unless otherwise noted, Scripture quotations are from *The Holy Bible, English Standard Version®* (ESV®) Copyright © 2001 by Crossway, a publishing ministry of Good News Publishers. All rights reserved

Italics in Scripture quotations are the emphasis of the author.

Contents

Introduction

The Reservoirs of Western Christianity

Most Christians agree that more people should be missionaries. We just don't agree on who those people should be. There's a good chance that you should be one of those people.

The premise of this book is to defend and qualify why YOU are one of those called to be a missionary. In fact, I wrote this book because I am troubled by the invisible barrier that stands between the majority of Western Christians and the commission to take the gospel to the world.

I don't mean that there is a barrier between Christians and the world. Quite the contrary! I find the average Western Christian to be surprisingly traveled and informed. The increased ease of transportation in recent generations has led to more believers in more churches visiting more mission fields than was previously feasible. I am always amazed by the number of people I encounter who have been to China, where my wife and I are church planters.

Additionally, the proliferation of modern media has raised the level of awareness of the world's condition to unprecedented levels. Communities in western nations are experiencing an unbelievable level of connection with foreign cultures via visitors, immigrants and refugees taking up residence in their midst. In Bowling Green, Kentucky, where my in-laws live, the public school system is being overwhelmed by huge numbers of children from non-English speaking families, from over sixty different language groups! Not bad for a dinky, traditionally-redneck town in the midwestern United States!

This is partly why it's so strange to me that some of the solutions most often proposed for addressing the need for worldwide missions are primarily informational in nature. The thinking of many seems to be that if Christians were better educated about the state of the world, those who *should* go *would* go. Thus, massive projects are undertaken to analyze and measure the remaining task of world evangelization, using the findings to repackage, restate and redefine the need in a way that might resonate with Western believers.

Sure, I've seen how this has certainly helped in creating awareness among American churches of the progress of the gospel in China—something that has surprised me again and again. It is unquestionable that some have in fact responded to these informative efforts and given their lives to go meet the need. But the gap between believers and the world still remains. Many of the most informed have not gone.

This is not a book filled with missions data. It's not a book of statistics about people with no access to the gospel or the growth of Christianity in various parts of the world. Excellent compendiums of such information are available elsewhere. You probably know most of the important numbers, anyway. If not, you certainly are aware that there are huge numbers of people in the world that have never heard the gospel.

Are believers totally lacking in missions fervor? No. An observation I will repeatedly come back to in this book is that there are probably as many people in this youngest generation of Christian leaders who feel the weight of the church's global mission as in any generation before it. There are many who truly long for God to receive glory from every tribe and language. They are not merely concerned with their communities and their churches—there is a consciousness of the global progress of the kingdom of God that thrills their souls.

So this book isn't trying to convince you that missions is a good thing. Though there may have been times in the church's history where believers may have been uninterested in the Great Commission, this is not one of them. The brothers and sisters in the churches I am privileged to associate with express nothing but appreciation and admiration for the work of a missionary. If anything, they go a bit too far in their applause, which, in my opinion, actually betokens the real problem—but more on that to come! The abundance of mission boards and organizations of virtually every evangelical stripe also reveals the high esteem in which the worldwide work of advancing the gospel is held. Yet in spite of all these positive sentiments regarding missions, there are huge harvest fields where the workers are either pathetically few in number or else absent altogether.

While I hope that everything said within its pages is established upon a solidly biblical framework, this book will not try to offer a comprehensive theology of missions. Again, evangelical churches have already benefited from several such excellent studies that demonstrate the God-glorifying significance of the Great Commission, and I could do nothing but express far more poorly what they have taught us so well.

Neither do I believe that this tragic gap can be viewed as just one aspect of a larger trend of evangelistic inactivity among recent generations of believers. There are many signs that this generation is in no short supply of men and women characterized by a holy ambition, a zeal for the gospel to be proclaimed to unbelievers, for justice to be done in human society and for the church of God to be edified.[1] The young blood flowing into Christian organizations, seminaries and healthy churches across the West is a testament to the vitality of this generation's commitment to live on mission.[2] But I do believe that it is not a zeal without bounds. For most of these young Christian leaders, their zeal will take them no further than the borders of their homelands.

Take, for example, the movement in recent years that has been dubbed the "young, restless and reformed," or the New Calvinism, a phenomenon that has been remarkable not only for its members' robust theological discipline and firm commitment to Scripture, but also their missiological zeal for church planting and culturally-contextualized preaching of the Word. If awareness of the mission's status, a passion for God's worldwide glory, and missiological energy in general were enough to bridge the gap between believers and the world, surely this movement would be in a prime position to send unprecedented numbers of young people to the world's harvest fields. Disappointingly, this has not yet been the case.

In fact, the idea of writing this book was spawned partly as a result of hearing some of the insiders of this movement express their frustration that more has not yet happened in this area. Here are a couple of examples:

In an interview with David Crabb, Bruce Ware, professor of Christian theology at Southern Baptist Theological Seminary, was asked to give his thoughts on the "young, restless and reformed" movement. From the front-row seat afforded him by his teaching position at a seminary where this movement is at its strongest, Ware gave high praise to what he perceived to be the movement's best characteristics. When prompted to give any thoughts of concern or encouragement, this is what he had to say:

> "I don't think there is yet a sufficient . . . passion within the hearts of this movement for taking the gospel to the world. You talk to these people and most of them are focused upon church-planting in North America . . . I can't help but think, why would God be doing this? I just cannot believe for one minute that the main reason He's raising up all these thousands of gifted young men is to penetrate North America. This has got to become a global missions movement." [3]

It wasn't long after that when I heard pastor and author Kevin DeYoung, speaking at the 2012 Together for the Gospel Conference, echo Ware's concerns:

> "I also believe . . . there are at least two very critical areas in which we have yet to show the sort of passion and enthusiasm and growth that we need. What are those two? One, I believe, is an earnest commitment to global missions. Stirring up ourselves, calling young people, some of you here, calling those in our churches to consider and go for the cause of the gospel to the unreached peoples of the world." [4]

So even in a modern movement that exhibits unusual missiological energy, there still is a kind of dam that keeps young Christian laborers pooled up in Western churches and keeps them from spilling out into the nations of the unreached. Even among those who are convinced of the necessity of church planting, gospel preaching and making disciples, there are remarkably few who choose to address those needs in places other than their homeland. Consequently, this is not a book about being missional—as if its average reader were apathetic about preaching the gospel at all. Almost certainly, you would not read a book like this in the first place unless you were already convinced of the critical value of Christians' evangelistic efforts.

Enough, then, about what this book isn't. Here's what it is:

First, this book is an examination of the gap between Western churches and missionary service. What exactly are the factors that keep young Christian leaders—who love Jesus and who love people—from being exported to the world? What leads to this stagnation in otherwise flourishing movements, as observed by Ware and DeYoung above? This is a diagnostic task requiring us to open the hood of Western evangelicalism and run some tests that we ordinarily might overlook.

Second, this book is an extended application of theology. There is certainly no new theological innovation to be found here (so the Inquisition can clock out early today), but I do believe that there is something about God and the gospel to be learned. What I hope to accomplish is to follow the threads of the theology you already believe to some of its logical conclusions concerning the world's unreached. I pray that those who love Jesus will find ways to apply the truth of his gospel in more radical ways to their lives.

Third, this book is an argument meant to be taken personally. In other words, much of what it has to say is directed at your will, the decision-making part of you. I deeply desire that something said here might, in its weakness, be used to effect a change of mind—specifically, that you would change your mind about going as a missionary. These are the parts that might upset some, because such argumentation necessarily implies that there might be something wrong with how you've chosen to live your life.

Fourth, this book is a presentation of a vision. I praise God that it is a vision that was passed on to me by others. It is a vision of churches and believers living with the Great Commission at their very core. Some of you may have met such a Christian before, or maybe even a group of them, and if you have, you know what a rare breed they are. They are not just people with a general evangelistic concern for unbelievers they happen to already know and love; they are people who live and court death to bring the gospel to the world's unreached millions. I have asked God to use this book to conform me to this vision, and I pray he does the same for its readers as well. May we see clearly the eternal gains that might be made for God's kingdom if the abundant reservoirs of Western Christianity were to surge forth to the arid ends of the earth!

If something written here helps to loosen the sediment or dislodge the debris that has dammed up young Christian leaders and all the other valuable resources of Western churches, the effort will have been worthwhile. I personally leave this project more sure than ever before that I want the embankment in my own heart to break open, that whatever portion of my energies I am holding back from the mission might flow out into the nations. That I may spend, and be spent, like so many great missionaries in the church's history, in joyful reenactment of the complete sacrifice of the greatest missionary who has ever lived.

1

Cards on the Table

How is the Great Commission essential for making sense of our world?

Not long before starting work on this project, I had a discussion with a tearful college student, Wei Tao, who is a member of one of the unregistered churches we've planted here in northeast China. For the last semester or so, Wei Tao has been receiving informal ministry training from his own pastor and the other pastors on our team. We have been encouraging him to consider giving his life to preach the gospel. Wei Tao has continued to exhibit a faithful, diligent, teachable and impassioned spirit, so we wanted him to wrestle seriously with the idea of serving full-time.

Breaking Your Mom's Heart

Somewhere along the line, Wei Tao found himself in a serious dilemma. His family is far from wealthy and most of his school bills have been paid by taking out loans. He'd just completed his sophomore year of college and the thought of continuing two more years, only to leave his major behind to prepare for gospel ministry, seemed wasteful of both time and money. So Wei Tao decided that if he was going to become a church planter, he would drop out of school early and begin to train.

To be honest, I wasn't sure how I felt about that. As a missionary in a city with millions of people who have never heard the gospel, I'd been pleading with God to bring Wei Tao into full-time church ministry. In fact, I'd prayed for men like him since years before our arrival in China. There is a desperate need for hundreds of young Chinese men just like Wei Tao to throw themselves into the work of the Great Commission. Needless to say, I was hardly objective about his decision to enter the ministry; I very much wanted him to drop out of school.

On the other hand, I was scared for him. I understood better than he could the hardships that would await him as a pastor of an unregistered Chinese church. And I was scared for my own sake, as I always am in these cases. This guy was about to cut his ties to the greatest security this life could offer him (in his country, the benefit of a college education), in large part because of my counsel to him. I felt enormously responsible for his making a decision that could potentially have disastrous consequences—not to mention the fact that I was afraid his parents might hire someone to rub me out! Like many Chinese families, they'd hitched their wagons to their son's educational prospects. Who knew how they would react to the news of their son quitting school to become a preacher of Christianity?

Which brings us back to our tearful discussion. After the church service the previous night, Wei Tao told me that he had made up his mind. He was going to join up and begin his training full-time. He went back to his dorm and called his mother (his dad isn't home often, as he travels for work). Naturally, she lost it. She wept and sobbed for hours on the phone, asking her son what kind of dangerous cult he had joined, what drove him to this kind of self-destructive behavior, and what did she need to say to make him see reason. Wei Tao's a good son, and it broke his heart to hear his mom carry on like that.

Now you see why I'm far more fearful of suffering persecution at the hands of angry parents than at the behest of the Chinese government! To the latter, I'm a subversive, but nothing a simple deportation wouldn't solve! To Wei Tao's mom and dad, though, I'm part of what turned their son into an uncontrollable, fanatical, cult-member disappointment. Wei Tao continues to plow forward in his commitment to serve as a minister of the gospel, but the barrage of emotional pressure from his family has not let up, either.

A Wartime Proposal

I tell you Wei Tao's story so that you know that I fully understand the consequences of what I'm proposing in this book. I am going to plead with you to think about becoming a missionary, and it might come across a little harsh at times. But I hope you won't think that I would at all trivialize the sacrifices that stand between you and such a commitment. The price tag for the proposal in this book is enormous. I get that. They don't make dumpsters big enough to hold all the stuff this book will suggest you chuck!

Believe me, I'll still plead, because the same truths that drive me to take part in crushing a poor Chinese family's worldly aspirations are just as true when they come to you and me, and much more so. These truths tell us that it is no time of leisure and peace in which we live today. It is a time of such gravity that those who have families are told to live almost like those who don't (see 1 Cor. 7:29). In other words, it is a time of war.

A time when even our lives aren't a sufficient token of the value of our cause.

What kind of a war is it?

It is a war instigated (unconsciously, in some cases) by the peoples of the world who, though created to be the greatest of God's worshipers, have taken up arms against their Creator and King. They have cursed Him and denied His right to rule them. They have robbed from Him all the honor and glory that He is due, even as they thanklessly gorge themselves on his gifts. They despise His will and insult His perfectly holy and wise character (see Luke 19:12-27; Rom. 1:18-23; James 4:4).

They have lied about Him and called it "philosophy." They have mocked Him and called it "entertainment." They have disobeyed Him and called it "culture." They have ignored Him and called it "politics." They have tried to manipulate Him and called it "religion."

This treason is universal. There remains no nation, no culture, no language, no tribe and no city loyal to the banner of the rightful King. Nowhere are His ensigns welcome; nowhere is His law observed. In rejecting His just governance, every corner of the earth has embraced and exalted its own greedy warlords, sadistic dictators and foolish aristocracy to rule in His place. Rebellion has brought not freedom, but enslavement (see Ps. 2:1-6; Eph. 2:1-3; Rom. 3:9-24).

Despite the confidence of these usurpers and those who put their trust in them, it is not possible that their rebellion can stand forever. They are doomed. The King is as mighty as He is just, and the wicked acts of every rebel will surely come into judgment. There will be no bunker or cave (or grave) deep enough to shield them from the righteous beam of eternal justice. Every treasonous word, every traitorous deed will be revealed. Each of the false kings will be dethroned, dishonored and decimated. All who swore loyalty to them will become an eternal memorial to the King's just omnipotence (see Isa. 66:24; Rom. 2:5-8; Rev. 17:14).

This is the world where Wei Tao lives. Northeast China is just another rebellious district in the kingdom that rightfully belongs to God. Wei Tao can't pretend that there isn't a war going on. He can't act like his family and his city and his country and his world aren't living each day as willing conspirators in the most evil insurrection fathomable. Whatever else he may consider—the value of a college career, his family's ambitions and his own misgivings about ministry—he must not fail to take the war into account.

This is the world where I live. My eyes were first opened to the global scale of the war when I was fresh out of high school, working full-time and preparing for ministry with what I felt to be a sufficiently sober attitude. My buddy invited me to a midweek service at a microscopic church in Cincinnati to hear an Australian missionary speaker. (He had me at "Australian," as I'd gladly listen to an Australian give play-by-play instructions on paint drying!) We arrived late and tried in vain to enter the tiny, nearly-vacant auditorium without making a scene—but we hadn't missed the Australian! His only points of discussion (that I can remember, anyway) were about the nations of the world, which he indicated one at a time on a large world map he had set up in front of the pulpit. He talked about multitudes of people, of diverse languages, religions and races, who were living in active rebellion against God and in ignorance of His revelation. I left that little church looking at the whole world in a new way: as a battlefield.

You, too, live in this world at war. Can any loyal subject of the King not recoil in horror at the treason of sin? Can the King's own children be unmoved by the idols sitting on His throne? The war for God's worship demands our action. What can we do with our lives that will help put down this wicked rebellion and restore God to the throne over the peoples of the world?

Here's an example that is a little closer to home: When a nation finds itself desperately struggling for victory in any global conflict, every citizen is called upon to forfeit his freedom to live a normal life. As in our previous World Wars, food is rationed. Factories are converted for military purposes. Hospitals make space for wounded soldiers. Train stations become air-raid shelters. Housewives go to work in assembly lines. And of course, young men are deployed to the trenches. Those expectations in life that seemed so reasonable before war broke out suddenly seem self-centered, impractical and unpatriotic. What could be more reasonable than a young scholar planning to attend college? What could be more natural than a family gathering for a feast? What could be more normal than a business owner trying to make a profit? Yet in wartime, all bets are off. Commodities become luxuries. Aspirations give way to obligations. Restfulness is exchanged for watchfulness.

Thus, the first thing that we as believers must keep in mind as we plan our lives is the worldwide scope of the war against God. The lifestyle of Christians in any society ought to be in sharp contrast to the surrounding cultural norms, and not just in a moral way. We can't simply live as we please while a spiritual war rages around us. Even seemingly insignificant decisions must come under careful scrutiny. Christian life-planning starts out by saying, "What can I do to help in the worldwide war for God's worship?" Again and again, we surrender our interests, passions and dreams, reminding ourselves, "Yes, but there's a war on." There must be rationing. There must be training. There must be vigilance. Peacetime will come, but for now the war effort deserves our all.

But how can such a war as this be won? How can a rebellion as deeply entrenched as this be rooted out? How can we win back God's worship?

One Strange King

Just when it seems certain that God's righteous judgment must lash out and burn up every trace of the rebellion that contaminates his kingdom, there is heavenly silence. Where is the absolute, crushing grip of sovereign omnipotence? Reassured by His silence that the Creator King is either a myth or a weakling, the peoples of the world rejoice all the more merrily in their impostor kings. What exactly is God waiting for? Why entertain this treason a moment longer? Why not reclaim His glory and His throne (see Hab. 1; John 3:17; Rom. 3:25-26; 2 Pet. 3:3-9)?

But then, in a small town, a baby is born, unnoticed by all the peoples of the earth. For what is He next to the great impostor kings they have erected? He has no wealth, no power, no status. But this tiny child who enters the world in humble weakness is the beginning of the rebellion's end. For though they don't recognize Him, He is the rightful King over all the peoples of the earth (see Matt. 2:2; John 12:31; Phil. 2:5-7; 1 John 3:8)!

He grows up and perplexes the rebel kingdoms. Who is this man? He is more like a king than any they've bowed to—nature itself obeys His command. And He Himself bows to no other king: not to Nationalism, Individualism, Tradition, Family, Religion or Wealth. But when the peoples of the earth put Him to trial, and the kings of the earth condemn him, He allows Himself to be butchered like an animal, nailed to a piece of wood. The peoples gather to sneer at the irony, and then return to their respective kings' banners. But of course, Death itself bows the knee, and on the third day the Creator-turned-Man steps out of His tomb (see Matt. 4:8-10; 8:27; 27:42; Mark 1:27; Acts 2:24; 4:27-28).

What happens now? Is this the moment, we wonder, when the righteous judgment blasts the rebels? Will the kingdom be restored now? We might think so. Their treason is complete. Given the opportunity, they have murdered their King. Instead His followers receive a commission to tell all the world, every rebellious clan, that the deadly demands of justice have been met! Mercy and restoration are now available for every traitor! How is this possible (see Matt. 28:18-20; Acts 1:8; Rom. 3:21-26)?

When the unrecognized King hung on the cross, the judgment, the perfectly just punishment saved up for every treasonous act and treacherous word and traitorous thought, did finally lash out and burn. Its beam, however, was confined to and concentrated on, not the rebels, but Jesus the rightful King. He suffered in their place so the rebels might be saved from themselves (see 1 Tim. 15). The reason for the mysteriously absent judgment becomes beautifully clear: God is rich in mercy. What He wanted from the start was to graciously redeem a nation of ex-rebels from their own treason. They would live forever to worship Him as their Savior (see Rom. 3:25; Eph. 2:3-5; 1 Pet. 2:9, 24; 1 John 4:10)!

So Jesus tells His disciples that He is sending them to the world, just as His Father had sent Him. He sends them to bring life to the world in His name. Just as the treason is universal, so is the commission. His redeemed ones are to take the news that the King welcomes the rebels to repent and be reconciled to Him. With all provisions made on their behalf, He asks that they spread this news as extensively in the kingdom as the rebellion's contamination has pervaded. The righteous judgment still looms over the head of every recalcitrant traitor, and the peoples of the kingdom will assuredly one day bow before Him. In the meantime, however, grace is available to whosoever will (see John 20:21; Acts 2:40; 2 Cor. 2:14-17; 5:18-21; Eph. 2:8-11; Phil. 2:9-11; Heb. 2:1-3; 10:19-22).

And that's the other half of the truth about the world where Wei Tao (and every single one of us) lives. The Great Commission tells him that this is a glorious age of unthinkable mercy. He is a redeemed rebel. He attained a reconciled status via the ministry of another redeemed rebel. And now, he bears the only hope for redeemed rebels all around him in northeast China, in central China where his family lives, and in the uttermost parts of the earth. So again I ask, how can he not live in the light of these truths? Is his decision to drop out of school or to become a church planter so radical when you consider the time in which he lives?

I'm in this same glorious age. A few months after my eye-opening experience in Cincinnati, my same friend (who's now a missionary in Morocco) invited me to go to Peru to train with a veteran missionary there. Not surprisingly, I fought him more on that than the trip to Cincinnati (there were no promised Australians, for one thing). But he got me there, and when I arrived, I saw things that blew my mind. I saw churches filled with believers rejoicing over their state as reconciled rebels and young men and women who were volunteering to go anywhere in the world as ministers of reconciliation. They believed the provision of the cross was enough for the whole world, and they ached to bring glory to the King who redeemed them. In other words, they couldn't experience this grace without their joy overflowing to the world. I felt that I, too, could no longer do so.

Most of all, this is also *your* age. Think for a moment about your plans for the future. What is the driving force behind them? As you're reading a book like this one, I'm quite sure your plans seem very reasonable and respectable to most people; but have you given sufficient consideration to the time in which you live? The Great Commission announces that an age of unprecedented grace has dawned. Christians who choose to live for a different purpose aren't simply disobedient—they're behind the times! Because of Christ's accomplished work, we aren't solely in a time of war; we are in a time of victory! Now is not the time to tremble in fear of the world's darkness and rebellion! It is the time to shine light into that darkness!

This is the time in which you have been privileged to live. Blessed are your eyes, for they see. Blessed are your ears, for they hear (see Matt. 13:10-17). Can you make the major decisions in your life—what job to take, where to move your family, what to do with your money—without even considering the ramifications of this unique period of grace? Sure, it's lasted two thousand years, but there's still much ground to be won, and we aren't guaranteed a single day more! What can you do to put down the rebellion of sin and restore worship to the One who alone deserves it? You have been sent forth by Christ with a guarantee of His power attending. With this confidence alone, you can march into the darkest places on the earth with the glorious news of reconciliation.

Lives Forever Changed

These are truths that demand our lives. So please understand as you read the rest of this book that this is why I plead. I live in one of thousands, if not millions, of rebel outposts around the world. The need surrounds and often overwhelms us.

Obviously, my retelling of a story that you know so well isn't enough to prove that you should *1) quit whatever you're doing* and *2) become an overseas missionary.* There are still so many questions and protestations left for us to wrangle. Why you and not someone else? Aren't there other noble endeavors for believers to pursue? Why there and not here? Are you qualified to be a missionary? And wrangle with all these we shall. In the pages to come, my hope is to show you the many reasons that you should personally consider missionary service. I certainly realize that not every Christian belongs on a foreign field, but I will rejoice if anything written here is of any use in leading many more of God's redeemed rebels to engage more fully with the worldwide war and the corresponding ministry of reconciliation.

I wanted to start off in this first chapter where we agree: the gospel has done something so monumental in the world that we can never live in the same way again. There's a war on, and God has miraculously brought us to His side of the battle lines. So there's no getting "back to normal" for believers. All our plans are merely provisional. While our list of agreements may extend no further than this page, I hope we agree that, whether or not you're supposed to be a missionary sent to speak peace to the rebels in some far-flung battlefield of this global war, nothing could be more reasonable than for God to ask that of Wei Tao, of me or of you.

2

The Great Commission Paradigm

Does the Commission summarize the entirety of the Church's mission?

Now the eleven disciples went to Galilee, to the mountain to which Jesus had directed them. And when they saw him they worshiped him, but some doubted. And Jesus came and said to them, "All authority in heaven and on earth has been given to me. Go therefore and make disciples of all nations, baptizing them in the name of the Father and of the Son and of the Holy Spirit, teaching them to observe all that I have commanded you. And behold, I am with you always, to the end of the age."
– Matthew 28:16-18

In the next few chapters, I want to turn our attention directly to the Commission itself. This command seems to be one of the last things that Jesus passed along to his disciples before leaving the earth. And these words have been something of a rallying cry for missionaries for hundreds of years. So if we're trying to decide whether or not we should go to the other side of the world as missionaries, what better place could there be to start our investigation?

A Branch or the Trunk?

There have been some in the history of the church who have believed that Christ's last command no longer applies to us,[5] but this seems now to be an extreme minority opinion among evangelicals. While the case for the Commission's relevance to us has been handled by far more adept writers than myself, I want to focus here on something else—namely, the significance of the Commission for the church. To put it as a question, is the Great Commission supposed to be paradigmatic for the church, or is it just one more item on a list of things the church is supposed to do? Is it a branch on the tree, or is it the very trunk? If Christ meant His last command to serve as a sort of overarching corporate purpose statement for believers, then the major thrust of our earthly lives must be oriented toward the goal of worldwide disciple making. If, on the other hand, the Great Commission is one goal among many, there may be important goals and plans and tasks in our lives that will not fall under the rubric of "mission."

First, let me acknowledge that there are definitely a variety things that believers are commanded to do. I have no intention of attempting to reduce the whole of a Christian's actions to evangelism. Instead I mean to echo theologian Wayne Grudem when he says in his book *Making Sense of the Church: One of Seven Parts from Grudem's Systematic Theology*, "This evangelistic work of declaring the gospel is the primary ministry that the church has toward the world."[6] Meaning, the Great Commission is the great project and goal of the church's work on earth. As a church, our ministry, the primary thing we are working toward, is making disciples out of nonbelievers.

The church relates to disciple making the way a hospital relates to healing, the way a restaurant relates to serving food, the way a power company relates to providing electricity, the way a school relates to teaching, the way a fire department relates to putting out fires, the way a baseball team relates to getting on base. It's what we do. There are other things we find ourselves doing at times, of course. For example, a doctor might rearrange his office furniture or a fireman may break down walls to free a morbidly obese person. A Christian must pay bills, get a haircut and change his oil. But we don't define our mission on earth by these other things, nor do we measure our success by them. A believer can no more opt out of disciple making than a podiatrist can get around feet.

But I understand that there are believers (many of whom do care about missions) who do think that disciple making is just one dish of many on the table. So below, I want to share a few reasons why I think this position is inadequate and why I maintain that the command of Christ is paradigmatic for the church's work in the world. (If you're a believer who's already convinced that the Great Commission should be central to our understanding of the church's earthly mission, feel free to view this as a reminder of vital truths).

Reasons to think of the Great Commission as paradigmatic for the church:

The Positioning in the Biblical Text

The command to propagate the gospel to all of humanity figures in prominent places in the Gospels according to Matthew and Luke. Matthew, with all that he tells us about Jesus, chooses to conclude his writings, not with the ascension, but with the most well-known version of the Lord's Commission. The resurrected Lord informs His followers that the Father has made him the highest authority in the universe (see Matt. 28:18)! By virtue of that authority, then, He commands them to go out into the world and multiply His followers, initiating them into a life of discipleship by baptism in the triune name of God, and teaching them to live obediently to Christ (see Matt. 28:19-20). Jesus' closing words (and the end of Matthew's Gospel account) are a promise that His disciples can count on Him to be powerfully present with them until the very end (see 28:20).

Taken in its entirety, Matthew's Gospel has demonstrated that Jesus is the promised Messiah and that His kingdom, composed of all those who become His disciples, has already dawned, and is destined to spread throughout the unbelieving world. Thus, the book ends here, with the Lord's declaration that all the authority in the universe is firmly in His grasp, and His subsequent command for the disciples to continue the work of making disciples out of the unbelieving masses. The reader of Matthew's Gospel closes the book knowing not only that Jesus inaugurated a kingdom, but knowing what he or she is expected to do to continue this kingdom project.

Similarly, Luke wraps up his testimony to Christ by recording His final commands to His small band of disciples before leaving the earth (see 24:44-49). Several of Luke's significant emphases come together in these last "marching orders." First, Christ reminds them that the events of His cross and resurrection were sovereignly decreed; if they have any doubt about that, they need only remember the words of the Old Testament (see 24:44; also 24:27). Then He provides them with the insight to see this sovereign design in Scripture, presumably calling their attention to specific texts that showed the Messiah's rejection and ultimate triumph (see 24:45-46). This Old Testament instruction prompts a profound hermeneutical enlightenment that will characterize the rest of their teaching careers (see, for example, Peter's speech in Acts 2).

But Jesus' scriptural exposition doesn't stop there! There is something else to God's prophesied plan, something that includes them integrally. He goes on to show them that the Messiah's message of forgiveness is to be offered to all nations, starting from Jerusalem (see Luke 24:47). Therefore, the mission on which they are about to embark is, like His own death and resurrection, sovereignly decreed and destined to achieve its purpose! This also reminds the reader of all Luke's repeated insistences that this Messiah is here to do something more than bring Israel political liberty; He has come to be the blessing to the nations, something prophesied long ago (see 2:29-32).

With that, Jesus tells them to hold tight until they receive the promised Spirit, and then He ascends (see 24:49). The reader is left with a distinct impression of incompleteness. The resolution of Luke's Gospel account has the tension of a cliffhanger! The disciples are waiting for the empowerment that will set in motion a gigantic initiative. Luke's historical witness ends with a trajectory pointed toward the unbelieving nations, a trajectory that he immediately resumes in the first chapter of Acts.

> He presented himself alive to them after his suffering by many proofs, appearing to them during forty days and speaking about the kingdom of God.
>
> And while staying with them he ordered them not to depart from Jerusalem, but to wait for the promise of the Father, which, he said, "you heard from me; for John baptized with water, but you will be baptized with the Holy Spirit not many days from now."
>
> So when they had come together, they asked him, "Lord, will you at this time restore the kingdom to Israel?" He said to them, "It is not for you to know times or seasons that the

Father has fixed by his own authority. But you will receive power when the Holy Spirit has come upon you, and you will be my witnesses in Jerusalem and in all Judea and Samaria, and to the end of the earth." (Acts 1:3-8)

Here Luke backtracks only briefly to let us see the disciples' misunderstanding of the mission, and to provide a bit of context for the command as it came to the disciples. The disciples ask Jesus if this is the time for Israel's kingdom restoration (see Acts 1:6). Is this when the throne of Jesus will start to look more recognizable to the Jewish people? Can they now expect Jesus to revive God's chosen people and lead them to worldwide pre-eminence? Jesus' response is intriguing (1:7). He doesn't sharply rebuke them. It's not even a clearly negative answer! This seems to hint that their idea isn't too far from the right one, though their misunderstanding is a serious one. Jesus says simply that it's not for them to know the "when" of God's kingdom plan. The earthly enthronement of Christ, as they were envisioning it, was not the next thing on the calendar.

Before we see how close they were to the right idea, notice that the disciples here are searching for a paradigm. Their question is about the fundamental nature of the new age that dawned at Christ's resurrection. They are certainly right in understanding that the role and function of God's people in the earth has undergone a change—they just don't know what the change is! What will they be doing now, if not ruling with Christ over Israel? The bigness of their question shows us the all-encompassing nature of Jesus' answer in verse 8! They're not asking Jesus to explain one aspect of the Christian life. Instead, they are asking for Jesus to provide them with an encapsulation of their mission and identity in this age. And He gives it to them!

The mission for the newborn church will be to serve as His witnesses to all the earth (see 1:8). It's as if Jesus says, "Not that paradigm, but this paradigm!" This is how close the disciples were. As their witness expands from the historic capital of the Jewish nation, throughout the traditional boundaries of Israel, into the estranged Samaritan territory and beyond to the remotest parts of the earth, God's chosen people are in fact being revived and restored to previously unknown glories! No, the kingdom doesn't look much like the disciples' Jewish roots had taught them to imagine. For that matter, the people of the kingdom were to be pretty different than they expected, too! But make no mistake, it was the Son of David's kingdom, and He would possess the earth (see Ps. 2:8)! This was the paradigm for all that is to come for the church in the book of Acts.

So beyond simply *what* Jesus says about the mission, *where* He says it shows us the overarching nature of the disciples' commission. At these key places in the New Testament record, Jesus presents the proclamation of the gospel as the church's paradigmatic agenda in this world. The Great Commission does actually serve as a summary of what the church is to work for in this age.

The Unfolding Direction of the Book of Acts

The Acts of the Apostles give us further evidence for seeing the Great Commission as paradigmatic for the church, because the events that Luke recounts for us show the disciples' (not just the apostles') commitment to the centrality of missions.

Luke continues on with the disciples receiving the gift of the Spirit and immediately beginning to fill Jerusalem with the gospel message (see Acts 2-5). There is an initial harking back to the command of Christ, as Jewish men from nations all over the world hear the gospel preached by the apostles on Pentecost (see 2:5). As Luke describes the continued ministry of the church, he frames each episode in his account with phrases that show the progress of the mission: increase in the volume of the proclaimed Word and increase in the number of disciples (see Acts 2:47; 4:4; 5:14; 6:7). These recurring "progress reports" reveal that the church in Jerusalem is doing exactly what Christ sent them to do. The story Luke has to tell is of the first generation of disciples carrying out the Great Commission.

After the stoning of the early church's bold preacher, Stephen, in Acts 7, the mission only becomes clearer! It is really in Acts 8 that the notion that the Great Commission is limited to the ministry of the apostles really unravels. As a result of the persecution sparked by Stephen's death, everyone *except* the apostles go everywhere preaching the Word (see 8:1)! And the most prominent of these missionaries, Philip the evangelist, is no apostle either! Philip becomes the first to preach the gospel to the partly-Jewish and to the completely non-Jewish: the Samaritans and the Ethiopian eunuch (see 8:5, 27). This shows us the veins of the gospel beginning to stretch out even further from Jerusalem.

Then, of course, Paul comes on the scene. He and his team—including Luke—push the gospel out further yet, planting churches in key cities and creating main arteries for its flow to even more remote areas of the known world (see chapters 13-28). Luke's point seems clear. He has drawn a fairly straight line right down from the departing command of the risen Lord to the boats he is riding in with Paul. The story of Acts is most simply seen as the story of the gospel's advance. For a book entitled "The Acts of the Apostles," some of those apostles get precious little time in the spotlight, and after about midway or so, it seems to be a one-man show. Why? Because for Luke, the progress of the church is related most critically to their obedience to the Great Commission, and he has chosen to tell the story of the church accordingly.

In other words, making disciples of all nations is not to be seen as one of the church's valuable contributions to the world. Acts portrays the gospel mission to the world as the most basic element of the church's mission in the world.

The Self-Evident Need for Continued Work

As noted, the church today has reached a wide consensus that the Great Commission was not limited to the apostles, but remains binding for modern believers as well. While we will not linger to discuss them fully, there are strong arguments to defend this position. For example, the promise of the Lord's continued presence to the end of the age (see Matt. 28:20) suggests that the command bolstered by this promise will remain in effect until the same time. Jesus promises to be with us the whole time we are making disciples of the nations—until the end of the age.

It is here that I want to draw your attention to yet another reason often given for believing in the perpetuity of the Commission: namely, that the apostles did not complete it. The unbelievable thing is really not that the apostles failed to do something they were supposed to do (Scripture makes their fallibility very plain). The unbelievable, unacceptable thing is that God would fail to do something that He was supposed to do!

As important as it is for us to realize that the Great Commission is a command for us to obey, it is equally important that we acknowledge it to be part of God's unshakeable plan! A contrast of Matthew and Luke's versions of the Commission reveals that the evangelization of the world is both a sure thing decreed by God and a mandated work dependent upon the obedience of the disciples (see Matt. 28:18-20; Luke 24:45-49; Acts 1:8). We will be His witnesses to the end of earth. Yet we must proactively go and make disciples. The sure declaration of God concerning the evangelization of the world must therefore lead us to believe that the apostles' incomplete task is far from the end of the mission's story. God will not leave the Great Commission incomplete.

All of these reasons lead us to a certainty that the baton of the Great Commission has been passed on to us from the church of generations past; but there is more to it. These reasons intimate the priority of world evangelization. How? Well, it's in the nature of purpose statements to have a longer shelf life than just one generation. If the founder of an organization wants to ensure that his organization maintains a desired trajectory for, say, two thousand plus years, he will craft a purpose statement that explains what the organization should do as long as it is in existence. That way, generations to come will be able to look back to that statement and grasp the vital core of the organization's mission. If the statement is given in such a way that the first generation seems to fulfill all of its stipulations, later generations will doubt whether the founder had something else in mind for them to do!

So if Christ meant His last command to be taken as a purpose statement for the church in future generations, it would not be surprising that it would remain in effect, not completely finished, two thousand years later. This alone is not proof that the Great Commission is central to the church's purpose on earth, but it is exactly what we would expect to find if it was! Thus, taken with the other reasons, the uncompleted status of the Commission leads us to elevate it to the role of "mission."

The Testimony of Church History

Let's look at one more argument for the centrality of the Great Commission before we move on. If we allow ourselves to view missions as a fairly recent development in church history, it will naturally be difficult for us to accept that it is really a statement of the church's purpose on earth. How could something that only came into existence in the last couple hundred years truly be a pillar of the church? A survey of church history reveals just the opposite: that whenever in church history there has been a deepening commitment to the truth of the gospel, there has also been more zeal for making disciples of all nations. To discover the high points of Christian missions, one need only search for those times and places in history where churches strove diligently to conform themselves to Scripture.

In her volume on missions history, *From Jerusalem to Irian Jaya*, Ruth A. Tucker writes, "But from its very inception Christianity was different from all other religions. The command to go forth with the good news was the very heart of the faith."[7] The mission to the peoples of the world was not just a peripheral feature of the Christian lifestyle, it was part and parcel of believing the gospel itself! Tucker goes on to quote Stephen Neill: "Every Christian . . . was a witness . . . nothing is more notable than the anonymity of these early missionaries."[8] She also quotes John Foxe: "In that age every Christian was a missionary . . . everyone who had experienced the joys of believing tried to bring others to the faith."[9]

Other historians concur that it was not a few people extraordinarily committed to missions who really contributed to the steady growth of Christianity in its infancy. Rather, it was realized by a commitment to discipleship that characterized the early church at large. Church historian Justo Gonzalez writes, "In truth, most of the missionary work was not carried out by the apostles, but rather by the countless and nameless Christians who . . . traveled from place to place taking the gospel with them."[10] Sociologist Rodney Stark's book *The Rise of Christianity* says, "Mostly the church spread as ordinary people accepted it and then shared it with their families and friends and the faith was carried from one community to another in this same way."[11]

But my favorite quote about this comes from the pen of Celsus, the ancient critic of Christianity. "Their aim is to convince only worthless and contemptible people, idiots, slaves, poor women, and children."[12] His complaint—though far from objective—shows that average Christians were engaged in proselytization.

There's no room here to talk about the multitude of notable missionaries whose testimonies have survived the centuries. Instead, we must press back to the point: as churches have become more attuned to the truth of the gospel, there has been a corresponding increase in zeal for missions. Let me address briefly what some would call a glaring hole in that theory.

The Protestant Reformation was a time of great upsurge in church purity across Europe, but it is often said that the theological slant of Calvin, Luther and the bulk of the other Reformers prejudiced them against the work of the Great Commission. Specifically, their view of God's sovereignty in election made them discount the necessity of worldwide disciple making. This unfortunate misconception deprives us of some rich missions history!

It is essential that we first take into account the spiritual condition of Europe when Luther, Calvin and the rest stood behind their pulpits. By our modern reckoning (and by Luther's and

Calvin's) their own lands were vast mission fields of nonbelievers in the gospel! How can we suggest that they didn't believe in missions? They were missionaries themselves! They preached, planted churches and wrote for the conversion of an enormous number of unbelievers all around them. Furthermore, Calvin demonstrated a fervent concern for unbelievers beyond the reach of his own church. He dispatched many dozens of churchplanters out of Geneva and into Catholic France, and many others were sent to places much further—four missionaries were even sent off to Brazil![13]

So, lastly, I suggest that the history of missions in the church gives us cause to suspect that the Great Commission should be considered the purpose statement for the church's work on earth.

Not Quite a Recipe

But even if it is agreed upon that the Great Commission should be taken as a purpose statement for the church's work on earth, we still haven't necessarily resolved all the questions the Commission raises. Not all purpose statements are equally specific or precise.

When I was in high school, I got my first job working at the fast-food restaurant Chick-fil-A. This chicken-frying chain restaurant has a wonderful-sounding corporate purpose statement: "to glorify God by being a faithful steward of all that is entrusted to us and to have a positive influence on all who come in contact with Chick-fil-A." But if on my first day of work, having never fried a chicken before, my training consisted only of reading that purpose statement, I would have been a little frustrated. The purpose statement doesn't even contain the word "chicken"! Not surprisingly, I didn't even know they had that purpose statement until well after my time there ended.

The point is, purpose statements don't always answer all our practical questions. They provide a framework, an overarching view of what is supposed to happen in an organization. In the church, that's how the Great Commission functions. It shows how the world should be different because the church is present. Though it may not helpfully describe what we are doing at every moment of every day, it is a useful way to remind ourselves of what the net product of our lives as Christians should be—disciples made out of the unbelieving masses. But there may be some details left for us to iron out.

I can think of four general categories of these kinds of details, questions that believers often have about the mandate of the Great Commission:

Questions of Duty - What exactly must be done?

Questions of Need - How much has already been done?

Questions of Gift - What can I do effectively?

Questions of Cost - How much must I do personally?

It is these questions that the next few chapters will address in turn. Hopefully, doing so will help us apply God's purpose statement more directly to our own lives and ensure that we are truly making this kind of an impact in the world.

3

Questions of Duty

What work is it that the Great Commission actually mandates?

Being a missionary in a closed country will make you eager to determine what exactly are the essentials of the gospel minister's duty. Here in China, for example, most everything we do as church planters is illegal. Last year we had a Sunday morning service broken up by a couple dozen police officers, and the Chinese pastors were taken in to the police station for questioning for a few hours. It's episodes like that that make you carefully consider what in ministry you can do without. For instance, can we stop evangelizing so openly? Or inviting unbelievers to church services? Or allowing foreigners to attend church? When ministry gets costly, we pause to ask, "What exactly is our mission here? What are the core actions prescribed by the Great Commission?"

Glory on His Terms

These questions are what I mean by "questions of duty." Many believers react to the Great Commission by saying something like, "Well . . . I think I'm doing that. Yes, I would say that what I'm doing counts as Great Commission work." There can be some confusion about just what it is specifically that Jesus is telling us to do. What are the bare essentials, the nonnegotiables of this ministry He has sent us to do?

It can be extremely nerve-racking to ask these questions about our duty, partly for the same reason that church planters in closed countries carefully dissect their mission. That is, if Christ is commanding me to do something that I'm not currently do-ing, there will almost certainly be a cost for me to change my life in that way. To make an extreme illustration, if the command to "go" in Matthew 28 is taken to mean that believers are never to lay down roots anywhere and must stay mobile like Romany Gypsies for the sake of disciple making, then this will obviously require most of us to completely overhaul our lives. Houses will have to be sold; luggage will have to be bought! When we talk about clarifying the command, there's always a fear that obedi-ence will require some uncomfortable changes to be made. So the questions that this chapter deals with are understandably sensitive ones. We all have a lot riding on the answers.

On the other hand, we should still want to get our duty clear because as believers we know that we have been created in Christ Jesus to do good works ordained by the Father Himself (see Eph. 2:10). We have an inner longing to obey His will on the earth. If He wants us in a mobile home, we want to be in a mobile home because we want to glorify Him! But that can only be done on His terms, not ours. So, in spite of the risks to our lifestyle, let us dare to ask the question in humility and with a worshipful desire to obey: *What exactly is it that Jesus is telling us to do?*

Specificity

How specific is the Great Commission? What stands behind those words "disciple," "all nations" and "witnesses"? Are they broad enough to include, for example, medical aid to a village in West Africa? How about large evangelistic rallies in American inner cities? Does the Commission include a missions trip to help build a church building in Nicaragua? Or what about just inviting coworkers to a church event? The truth is, you can find Christians working in all kinds of different ministries in the world, and all citing the Great Commission as the precept that undergirds their work! This might lead us to shrug and think, *"Well, the Great Commission is a little vague. Maybe it just means for us to be a force of good on the earth."*

I'm going to try my best to show that the Great Commission is actually quite descriptive as far as purpose statements go. It tells us specifically what it is that Christ expects to be done by His church for the duration of His absence. We must not think of Jesus here as saying something like, "Look, I want the world to glorify me—so you guys figure out a way to make that happen!" He didn't hold a meeting with His disciples to brainstorm ways to do good on the earth since sin and death had been finally conquered. Instead Jesus left behind a purpose statement that doesn't only tell us what He wants; it also tells us the "how," that is, the actual work we will do. The concreteness of the Commission's prescribed work also lays out some boundaries of the areas where we are not free to improvise or innovate.

Here is my own summary of what that work is, based on a blended reading of the multiple records of the Commission:

To proactively declare the gospel to unbelieving individuals in an effort to make them maturing disciples of Christ.

This is our duty. Nothing outside these lines counts as Great Commission work. This is the primary method that Christ has given us whereby we are to glorify Him on the earth. Let's break this summary down into its elements. That will give me a chance to both show you where in the text these phrases come from, and further define the terms used.

Declare the Gospel

As mentioned in the last chapter, from a certain perspective the Great Commission is simply undoable. We can't *make* a disciple. It requires a miraculous work of regeneration on the part of the Holy Spirit to awaken an unbeliever to the truth of the message that we preach. I can no more cause a Chinese person to put his faith in Christ than I can cause him to grow a foot. But this doesn't lead us to the fatalism that caused English Christians in the mid-1800s to encourage William Carey to put the thought of evangelizing the heathen out of his head since there was so obviously nothing he could do about it. Instead it leads us to hang the entire hopes of our mission endeavors upon the preaching of the Word. [14]

Why? Because the Word is referred to as the seed that the Holy Spirit causes to spring forth into new life (see 1 Pet.1:23-25). The seed of the Word does not always bring forth fruit (see Luke 8:11-15), but no fruit is ever brought forth without the seed. The advancement of the kingdom of God on the earth will never be an inch farther than the reach of the proclaimed Word of God. The Spirit has chosen the message of the gospel as the catalyst that creates a supernatural inner transformation within spiritually dead men.

Here, Luke's versions of the Commission become very helpful to us. Jesus decrees that His disciples will be His witnesses (see Luke 24:48; Acts 1:8). And what exactly are they witnesses of? Of Christ's redeeming life, death and resurrection. They have seen the new life that Christ's resurrection has inaugurated, and now they are to speak this testimony before a worldwide court. Luke says that with this testimony, they preach repentance and forgiveness of sins in the name of Jesus. In other words, we testify that it is only because of what Christ has done that anyone could ever be reconciled to God. Without knowledge of this message, no one will be saved.

This is both humbling and invigorating for a missionary. Although I can't convert a single Chinese person out of Buddhism, atheism or individualism, any Chinese person is still a perfect candidate for conversion. The salvation that is impossible for man is possible with God. The most energizing thing is that God did not choose to do this impossible thing without me. He has placed the message in my heart that can wake the dead, cold heart of any Chinese person!

This is the first step in understanding our duty. It means it's mission incomplete until we have spoken the news about Jesus to unbelievers. No one is exempt from the ministry of proclaiming the gospel, whatever your gifting or burden or walk of life. Christians cannot be divided into "those who preach the gospel" and "those who do good in their own way." Whether you're a stay-at-home mom or a deployed soldier or a nurse on a medical missions trip, we have not been obedient to our mission unless we are involved in speaking the content of the gospel (out loud, with words) to unbelievers. When we share what Jesus accomplished, we are fulfilling our life-giving mission.

Unbelieving Individuals

To whom, specifically, does the Great Commission send us to preach the gospel? Is this something that we even worry about, or are all targets of evangelism equally valid? This is one of the most loaded of the duty questions. It seems to pose the biggest threat to our comfort and security. If the answer to the 'who' question is simply *whichever unbelievers happen to currently be a part of my life*, then our lives can for the most part retain their shape. Any other answer is going to require some adjustments, however.

Luke expresses the answer to this question in geographical terms. He says that their witness will be given in Jerusalem, Judea, Samaria and the ends of the earth (see Acts 1:8). Yes, the disciples are first commanded to wait in Jerusalem for the empowering of the Spirit (1:4). But they have their final destination pre-saved in their internal GPS, ready to move as soon as the Spirit comes upon them. In Luke 24:47, Jesus gives the destination as simply "all the nations." However, Acts 1 shows the stages in which this will occur: from Jerusalem to Judea to Samaria and so on, until you run out of world.

Now this can be a tough bit of application for modern believers. After all, you most likely call some tiny fragment of the ends of the earth home. So where does the Great Commission point you? The most frequent explanation is that we start from wherever we find ourselves and move outwards from that point. Jerusalem is like your city, Judea's like your country or state, etc. This isn't a bad explanation, but I believe it can lead to some misunderstandings. There are some churches that largely ignore foreign missions endeavors, insisting that their priority lies with the evangelization of their Jerusalem before they concern themselves with the next step.

To realize the meaning of Jesus' words for us, I think it's helpful to put ourselves in the disciples' shoes at the time of Christ's ascension. The disciples are now witnesses to this incredible event, the resurrection of the Son of God. They have a corner on the gospel market. Beyond a couple hundred people, no one had heard the message they were commanded to preach. So how would they have understood Jesus' command to start in Jerusalem and move toward the nations? They would simply hear him saying, "Tell everyone. Yes, you will start in Jerusalem, but don't think it will end there. It will go on to places beyond. You will witness to all who don't yet have the gospel!" It's not so much that Jesus is prescribing a certain trajectory for evangelism (start at home and move out) as that He is piling up geographic locations to make them feel the enormous scope of the Commission (don't stop until all have heard). Therefore, I believe that Luke's versions of the Commission show us clearly that the "who" of our mission is those who don't have the gospel.

Let me pause here a second to clarify. There's a category of people today that did not exist at the moment in time when Jesus gave his Commission (or at least they were a tiny demographic). In fact, some of us may live in towns filled with this kind of person! Today, there are those who haven't heard the gospel (just like at the day of Christ's ascension), but there are also people who haven't listened to the gospel. They are the people to whom the gospel has already been preached, and they have rejected it. This is where deciding on the "who" gets tough. Does the Great Commission include our preaching to people who already have access to the gospel, or does our duty lie exclusively with those who are unreached?

Initially, it would seem like it does include them. After all, with the advent of radio, television and the Internet, there are remarkably few people in the world who have absolutely no access to the gospel. So it seems that all we ever do is improve someone's chances of hearing the gospel—whether they live in the midwestern United States or in Cairo, Egypt. Also, the Great Commission commands us to make disciples. It would seem that any non-disciple would be a candidate for those efforts. Thirdly, most who are Christians did not believe the gospel the first time they heard it; therefore, it is only natural that we would desire to give those who have heard and rejected the gospel another opportunity. God's longsuffering may yet save a gospel-rejecter.

But I maintain that there is a difference between preaching to those who have heard and those who have not. As a missionary in mainland China, I felt that difference before I could put it into words. In the time my wife and I have been here, we have been gloriously privileged to speak the gospel to so many who have truly never heard. Slowly, we came to realize that the Commission is a command to go hunting, not to go trapping. It is a command to go, not a command to wait. When trapping game, you set the snare, lay some bait and come back later, hoping you caught something. The hunter, though, is hungry now! He can't wait! So he proactively tracks the game and fires weapons until he kills something. There are some evangelistic tools that are like traps in that they create a latent potential for the people in a certain place to hear the gospel—provided they come to a website, read the literature left at their door, see the church sign, hear the radio advertisement, buy the book, etc.

That is NOT what the Commission commands. Though of course all of those things may at times be wonderfully productive, our duty remains undone no matter how many traps we have laid. What we should be looking for with every unbelieving individual in the world is an opportunity to speak the gospel to him or her as a piece of news he or she may then accept or reject.

The example of the apostle Paul also implies that the Commission points us mainly to those who have not heard. His short stays in many towns imply that he was not as concerned with providing a repeated witness to the gospel in a certain area as with moving on to areas where people hadn't yet had an opportunity to hear (e.g. Thessalonica, Berea and Athens in Acts 17). Consider, too, his willingness to pronounce the frightening judgment "your blood be on your own heads" to those who with understanding spurned the invitation of the gospel (Acts 18:6). In this and other places, it appears that Paul views his preaching of the gospel to those who have not heard it in some sense as clearing himself of responsibility for their souls (see 13:46, 51; 20:26; Rom. 1:14). So Paul's mission seems to have been centrally focused on those who lived in ignorance of the truths of the gospel.

If we measure in this way, the number of "Great Commission targets" in the world looks a bit different, doesn't it? There are clearly multiple millions who have never heard the message of Christ, while many others have heard and rejected it. The Commission seems to indicate that our primary duty lies with the former. This means that when we measure the amount of Great Commission work to be done in our homeland, it is vital to count something besides just people who don't *believe* the gospel. Doing so might lead us to believe our land is more needy than it really is! We must try to hit upon the number of people who have never *heard*.

Of course, there are likely at least a handful of people who have never heard the gospel in most every place in the world. But when it comes to dividing up the work, if there are more believers in the place you live than unbelievers who haven't heard, duty may call you to another place in the world. There are hundreds of places in China alone where that statistic is tilted terribly in the other direction. The few Christians that are there are facing odds of many thousands of *unheards* to one. Whereas in your homeland you might occasionally encounter someone who's really never heard the gospel message, that is the nearly unchanging moment-by-moment experience of missionaries in places all over the world. So duty might mean you need to move.

I heartily agree with missionary pioneer William Carey: "It has been objected that there are multitudes in our own nation . . . and that therefore we have work enough at home, without going into other countries . . . that [this] should supersede all attempts to spread the gospel in foreign parts seems to want proof. Our own countrymen have the means of grace, and may attend on the word preached if they choose it. They have the means of knowing the truth, and faithful ministers are placed in almost every part of the land . . . but with them [those in other lands] the case is widely different."[15]

One last note: In recent decades, there has been an increasingly popular missiological perspective that wants to reduce the range of "who" even further. We are told that when Matthew 28 commands us to make disciples of all nations, what Jesus means is some from each ethnolinguistic people group. That is, the Commission wants us to reach as many different kinds of people as possible, not just as many individuals as possible.

However, Jesus' references to "the nations" throughout the book of Matthew clearly refer to the mass of all unbelieving people as a corporate unit. In other words, the point is not "go make disciples out of all those specific individuals," nor is it "go make disciples out of all those various people groups," but rather it is "go make disciples out of that large unbelieving segment of the world's populace." Earlier in Matthew, Jesus had sent his disciples to preach to the Jews only, but none of "the nations." Then He foretold a coming era when His followers would preach to "the nations." Then finally in the Commission, Jesus tells His disciples that that time has now come, triggered by His glorious resurrection: "all the nations," not just Israel, are now legitimate targets for evangelism. Wherever there are unbelievers who don't have the gospel, we want missionaries on the case.

Proactively

My use of this word has already been clarified by the discussion of whom we are to go after. As I said, in many ways we are hunters, not trappers. We are not commanded to wait for the unbelievers to come to us, but we are to be out looking for them! A lifestyle that is not purposeful about proclaiming the gospel cannot be squared with the Great Commission. Here are a few more points before moving on.

What are we to make of the word "go" in Matthew 28? Does it mean that wherever we are when the Commission finds us, we should go to a different place? That would seem to lead to a lot of chaos and movement, but not a lot of disciple making. There are some who have said a better translation would be something like "as you are going, make disciples." The benefit of this translation is that it communicates to all Christians that they are to be on a disciple-making mission, no matter where they find themselves. But this translation also drains the imperatival force from the word "go."[16] This surely does some damage to the text, for many biblical scholars agree that Jesus is indeed mandating a change of location for His disciples as they are faithful to His mission!

Unfortunately, this popular interpretation may be seen as excluding us from a duty to proactively witness to unbelievers. It means we can just wait and see who we bump into! Perhaps we should ask, "Why and where are you going in the first place?" It is clear that Jesus isn't talking about *as you go about your day-to-day business*. Luke says the disciples (including us) are to be moving toward the ends of the earth.

No, there's a far better and more obvious way to understand "go." Every command to go (with the exception, I suppose, of banishment) has a target. Your pregnant wife says, "My water broke! I need to be driven to the hospital—GO!" and you know exactly where you're supposed to move. In the same way, Jesus commands us to preach the gospel to unbelievers—GO! So where do you run? Toward those unbelievers, wherever they may be!

The important thing is obviously not that you switch locations. What matters is that you are proactively seeking out unbelievers who have not heard the gospel, wherever they may be.

I say again, this might mean you need to move to India or Indonesia or Indianapolis. The mandate of Christ precludes us from making our home wherever we desire. Christians cannot lay deep roots anywhere. The Commission leaves no place for some stubborn geographical attachment that refuses to leave a house even when a hurricane is imminent. It leaves no room for that antisocial preference that leads one to isolate him-or herself in rural retreats. It excludes that dyed-in-the-wool patriotism that despises the lifestyles of other cultures, as well as that peculiar pride in being ignorant of all outside the view of one's own porch.

We are sent to the world's people, and when we run low on preaching targets in one locale, we must sacrificially move on to the next. Christians have many other considerations about where we make our homes than school districts, crime rates, commute times and distance from the beach.

You could say that "go" is about the priority of our duty. We may only stay put as long as we have our hands full of work. This seems to be the best way to understand the continual mobility of Paul. Cities were much smaller then, and a powerful preacher like Paul would run out of *unheards* before too long. You, on the other hand, may go to a megacity in Pakistan and go the rest of your life without running out! But one thing is certain: if you are in a place where the believers far outnumber the *unheards*, you should probably move. We may not default to "here" as home, but must with the Moravian reformer Count Nicolaus Ludwig von Zinzendorf say, "The world is the field and the field is the world; and henceforth that country shall be my home where I can be most used in winning souls for Christ."[17]

Maturing Disciples of Christ

And now we come to the product of our duty. What is it that we're trying to make out of the raw material of unbelievers? Disciples. Followers of Jesus. Most basically, this refers to someone who has responded in repentance and faith to the message we proclaim. But why does Jesus say we are to *disciple* unbelievers rather than just convert them or convince them?

In the previous section, we said that we have actually fulfilled our duty if a person hears but does not accept the gospel. But in the event that someone does respond to the gospel in faith, our duty takes on a new dimension. We must now assume the responsibility for this person to become a maturing follower of Christ. The word "disciple" shows us that we are not only aiming for people to make a profession of faith in Christ, to receive baptism or to become faithful members of a church. Rather, we want to see the authority of Christ stamped onto every facet of their lives. This means that evangelistic campaigns and rallies, correspondence teaching or inviting friends to church all fall short of the huge commitment that the Commission calls for. The Great Commission work involves teaching ALL that Christ has commanded us, and this is why I have included the modifier "maturing" in my definition of the Great Commission. We must continue our relationships with those who respond to the gospel, building them and guiding them toward perfection in Christ (see Col. 1:28). We will walk alongside them as they gain strength and stability in their obedience to the gospel.

Even in ministries within the church, we must be careful to assess our involvement with the Commission. Putting the word "ministry" after whatever it is we're doing doesn't exempt us from our responsibility to make disciples. You would think that as a missionary in a country with such a huge *unheard* factor, it would be almost impossible to stop making disciples of unbelievers. But an overseas church planter is just as likely to find his schedule full of non-disciple-making activities as anyone else! The directive of Christ should send us back to our day planners with an eraser. There is no acceptable substitute for this work of making disciples.

The decision to make maturing disciples out of unbelievers (and not just *heards* out of *unheards*) leads us inevitably to the church. Our duty is not merely to get the blood off our hands. The proclamation ministry would not be fulfilled just by driving into the middle of a neighborhood with a bullhorn and roaring the gospel message right through the walls of houses! Our goal is not just to check names off a list of people who haven't had a chance to hear yet. We do want all to hear, but we want them to do more than hear. We want them to see how the gospel changes a life completely. To do that, we need the church. A fellowship of believers who regularly meet to preach the Word, to pray, to worship, to observe communion and baptism. The new disciple will never be mature without a church family. The church is the body that will support and nurture his spiritual life for years to come.

It seems that recent generations of missionaries are heavily invested in trips, projects and goals that have little if any meaningful connection to local churches. This is tragic. It is virtually forfeiting any chance of accomplishing the disciple-making work prescribed by the Great Commission. There is certainly a superabundance of this type of missions endeavor in China, and it would be hard for me to portray accurately the utter uselessness of such plans. To divorce oneself from the fellowship of believers is tantamount to a decision to not make disciples at all!

Of course, this means that in many of the places where we will go looking for unbelievers, we will also need to be involved in the work of church planting. In places where there is no group of disciples gathering as a church, we shouldn't try to get by without one. Instead, we should consider how we can be the founders of the first church! Paul did not divide the work of preaching to unbelievers and planting churches, and neither should we.

So here we have the final piece of the duty given us by the Great Commission: making maturing disciples. We must not think our work complete when a person makes a profession of faith, and we must not think that we can merrily carry on our own private missions projects without the aid of a church. These resolutions will lead us over and over back to involvement with church planting.

The Irreducible Minimum

Let's review for a moment the Commission's answer to the questions of duty.

What exactly must be done? We must each declare the gospel to unbelieving individuals in an effort to make them maturing disciples of Christ.

As a missionary in China, there are times when I wish there was less to do. It would surely help us avoid some of our suffering. Still, whatever I might wish, this remains our duty. We all may occasionally wish to evade the ministry of disciple making and maintain our current lifestyle, location or loose affiliation with the church. However, we may not do so and claim obedience to the Great Commission.

In the next chapter, we will address the questions of need. To what extent is this disciple-making ministry happening in the world? Where exactly are these *unheards*?

4

Questions of Need

Where is there still a need for Great Commission work to be done?

Believers who do have a working understanding of their duty as given in the Commission often continue to wrestle with questions of need. They aren't sure if this essential work of disciple making is more needful in one place than another. I have had many long discussions with college students in the States who truly desire to do the work of the Great Commission, but who have serious misgivings about becoming missionaries. By and large, they have no measurement system in their head that helps them gauge the need in one place in comparison to another. They're not against foreign missions; they're just not sure they need to seriously consider such a thing for themselves.

Others just have a general feeling that there seem to be a lot of churches, believers and missionaries out in the world already. They know that more needs to be done in missions, the same way they know that their local radio station needs more people to call in with pledges to stay on the air. It just seems like so much melodrama, and the call for help usually falls on deaf ears. After all, there's no shortage of people in this world trying to drum up support for what they see as a critical need. Consequently, worldwide missions often gets shuffled into the same stack as reelection campaigns, blood drives, community volunteer work, school fundraisers and backing up your hard drive. Undeniably noble, but hardly priority.

So let's attempt to sketch out what the Great Commission tells us about the "need" of the world and what role we should expect to play in this mission.

How Many Places are Needy?

There are two errors we must be aware of in identifying the need for worldwide disciple making. We must exercise great caution here, especially as these errors are of that most deadly sort: the trendy. The first error is to say that everywhere in the world is equally in need of Great Commission work. With this error, we are told that geography doesn't matter; any place is as good a place to make disciples as another. The second error is exactly the opposite of the first. It says that there are actually very few places in the world where Great Commission work is still necessary. Which means both that the mission is near completion and that believers should focus their efforts on those last few pieces of the puzzle. Both of these views will lead us away from an accurate understanding of the world's need as portrayed by the Great Commission.

The first error was treated in some length in the last chapter, so I have just a few additional comments before moving on. Under what circumstances do believers wish it to be true that "all places are equally in need of missionaries"? In most cases, we say things like this to maintain the legitimacy of staying in a more "Christianized" environment. I recently heard this claim in a video made by a church planter going into an urban area in a midwestern American city. It was his way of convincing supporters that there was just as much of a need to help him get where he was going as to help someone going to Africa. This claim seems to insist that it makes every bit as much sense for us to stay where we are as to go to Burkina Faso.

Unfortunately, the Great Commission does not support the case. First of all, if the Commission is concerned with us getting the gospel to all unbelieving individuals in the world, does it not follow that those places with more unbelieving individuals (especially the *unheards*) are more in need of the gospel than those places where they are fewer?

You may say, "Ah, but there are many unbelievers still in my town. Isn't there a need for missionaries as long as there are any unbelievers remaining?"

No. There is not necessarily a need for someone to go (proactively) to this place to reach them. Why? Because need and demand are not the same. Here's an illustration. Let's say that only 5 percent of the people in your city have mailed a letter via the postal service in the past month. Does that mean, therefore, that there is a need for the postal service to drastically expand their operation in your city? Not necessarily. The questions we need to know the answers to are: Do citizens know where the post office is? Are they aware of the services that the post office provides? Is there anything besides their will that keeps them from mailing? Are they getting their mail out by another means? Until those questions are answered, we simply don't know if the postal service needs to expand, or if they have saturated the area and can do nothing more than continue to remind the community of their presence. Likewise, the continued presence of unbelievers in a place does not necessarily mean that there is a need for missionaries and church plants there.

Let me borrow another analogy that a good friend who serves in a Muslim country shared with me. There is an equal need of gospel preaching in all the world, in the same way that there is an equal need of food everywhere in the world! Yet this obviously doesn't mean that all people have an equal opportunity to get food! What this means is that we have a tendency to measure the wrong thing. No lost soul is more lost than any other, or more damned without the gospel. Sure, there are lost people everywhere! But, to extend the analogy, there are some who are starving in the storehouse, surrounded by food that they refuse to eat! Meanwhile, there are many millions who are perishing with no access to food!

Gloriously, in many places around the world, there are many churches, ministers and believers. The continued presence of unbelievers is no proof of the need for additional Great Commission efforts. Rather, we must see if the churches there are making their community aware of their existence and their message. Until those questions are answered, do we dare to say that there is as great a need in American towns with their dozens of churches as there is in the many cities in the Middle East with no gospel witness at all? For their sake, I hope not. Please understand that the possibility exists that you may be in a very un-needy place. May the Lord grant that we see the needy multitudes of unbelievers as he does!

By the way, this is not to say that all Christians should leave a place once a saturation point has been reached in disciple making. The church should remain an outpost of the gospel, continuing to inundate the community (and those who are added to the community year after year) with wave after wave of the message. Rather, it is to say that many should leave. Enough should be left to establish a perpetual witness, but the rest should move on to places of greater need. How many are needed, who stays and who goes are all questions to be pondered by the fellowship of missions-hearted believers in a particular place. With the Commission driving us, what else could we do but mobilize as many as we can afford?

The second error says almost the opposite of the first. It says that most places in the world have already been reached and that there is a relatively small number of places where Great Commission work is still needed. This thinking is closely related to the people groups theory mentioned in the last chapter. The basic premise goes like this: Since the Commission sends us to make disciples out of each people group, the Commission has been accomplished for those peoples in the world that have a sustained, indigenous group of believers.

This is challenging, because how many disciples must be made before we can check a people group off our unreached list? The number 2 percent gets thrown around a lot. This is supposed to be a kind of critical mass, when a group of believers is ready to take on responsibility for reaching their own ethno-linguistic grouping.[18]

The appeal of this reasoning is obvious. Rather than being a few billion gospel encounters away from completion, the church is only a few thousand people groups (and only 2 percent of each one) away from the finish line of missions. This theory often seems strategic. Focusing on the cultural and linguistic boundaries between peoples seems to let us know how far the gospel will travel unaided by missionaries. So we can prioritize our efforts and go to those culturally landlocked places to which the gospel will not naturally flow.

I don't think that many Christians who have embraced the people-groups theory have really grasped what a vast difference this perspective makes in the way manpower and resources are allocated. An examination of some of the revolutionary decisions made by missionaries and their boards since the advent of people-group thinking quickly reveals how widely divergent this path is from the traditional one. For example, many missions organizations no longer have any interest in sending missionaries to South American cities because most Latin American peoples have passed the 2 percent evangelical margin. Similarly, many missionaries in China are pushing toward the nation's minority people groups, distancing themselves from ministry with the Han Chinese, who make up 90 percent of China's population (and thus over 15 percent of the world's population!) because the Han, too, have crossed the finish line. They may not be to 10 percent, but they're past 2 percent, so it's on to the next. If, however, we maintain the traditional interpretation of the Great Commission, both Latin America and the Han Chinese would remain ideal targets for missionaries, as there are many millions of people in both groupings that have never heard the gospel.

This theory isn't nearly as practical as it sounds. To assume that the spread of the gospel is going to be hemmed in by a barrier as puny as culture or language is to overlook both scriptural and historical precedent. We are often told by this theory's advocates that missionaries are specialists who cross cultural barriers to bring the gospel to isolated people groups. This restriction of cross-cultural missions to one class of Christian worker is not borne out by the Bible or by experience. In Scripture, demolishing cultural barriers between ethnically different people is simply characteristic of the gospel (see Eph. 2:11-22). Furthermore, ordinary Christians are seen reaching across those barriers with the message of Christ, without any apparent special gifting to do so (see Acts 11:19-21). Not surprisingly, today we find that healthy churches in any of the world's cities (where otherwise distinct people groups tend to bleed into one another anyway) will often contain individuals from more than one of the people groups found in that city.

In conclusion, lest this chapter become overwhelmed by this one topic, let me affirm that the Great Commission points us to a need in the world wherever there are *individuals* who have not heard the message of the gospel. These places are not so few as the people group proponents would like us to think. Missionaries in some *reached* places in South America are still giving the gospel as fast as they can to people who haven't heard. They are in no danger of running out of *unheards* anytime soon. A large majority of Han Chinese have never heard. Many of the largest cities in the world, even in nominatively Christian nations, are in immense need of Great Commission ministry. Again, not only because they have large numbers of unbelievers or unchurched people (as could be said about practically *any* place on earth), but because they have huge numbers that have truly never heard the gospel message before.

So in your pursuit to answer the questions of need, don't fall into either of these errors. There are thousands of places where you could spend your life continually giving the gospel to *unheards*. But that is not the same as to say that all places are equally valid for you to plant yourself as a disciple maker. There may be some locations where your disciple-making efforts would make a much larger difference than they would if you were to stay where you are now.

Also, affirming that there is a spectrum of need doesn't eliminate the usefulness of measuring need any more than a spectrum of healthiness eliminates the usefulness of diagnosing illnesses. For instance, if you go see the doctor with an ailment, he's probably not going to shrug and say, "Well, you see, everyone's got one or two things wrong with their bodies. Nobody's 100 percent." Instead, if he's any doctor at all, he'll do his best to determine, by asking questions, making observations and running tests, if this ailment is a symptom of a serious illness. After making those determinations, he'll either prescribe treatment or tell you that you're in pretty good shape. We must do the same with every prospective mission field. We must analyze every "where" to determine how needy a place is and if it is a viable target for a believer's disciple-making efforts.

Vital Factors

So if these aren't the right ways to determine need, how are we to determine where the Great Commission is sending us? What measurements can be made that help us determine whether the place we're in is a good candidate for our disciple-making efforts, or if we should uproot ourselves? It might be helpful for us to think of this question in these terms: what would be the resulting condition of a given place if the directives of the Commission were being fulfilled? If we can formulate some idea of what that condition is, we could use it as a standard to which we could then compare various places around the world. Here are a few of the questions that can help us determine that standard:

- *What is the ratio of believers to unbelievers?*

- *In what condition are the existing churches?*

- *How many* unheards *are there?*

Once we've decided that the Great Commission is compelling us to give the gospel to as many unbelieving individuals as possible, it becomes immediately important to discover how many of those individuals are in a given place. In many places, simply asking how many professing believers are there will give you a very accurate picture of the need. For instance, there are many cities in North Africa, the Middle East, Central Asia, Southeast Asia, China and India where the number of professing believers in Jesus Christ is less than 5 percent of the population. Obviously, this means that any believer who calls these places home will have no trouble staying busy in the work of making disciples.

The state of affairs in these cities is in stark contrast to some places, predominantly in the West, where a majority of people claim to be Christians. If you live in a place like that, it might be time to consider a move to a needier location. This by no means denies that there remains a need for ministry among a population where most have heard the gospel before. Rather, it is to consider the workload to be borne by each believer in a place. Those Christians laboring to make disciples in cities where they make up a tiny sliver of the population will very likely never be able to complete the task of making the news of the gospel known to the millions who live around them unless missionary brothers and sisters come in from outside to join them in the work. This is why it is helpful to consider the ratio of believers to unbelievers in a place.

In many other places in the world, the number of believers is deceiving. There are some countries where practically everyone would claim to be a Christian, yet you would be hard-pressed to find even a few among them who could articulate the gospel. Often this is because their religious persuasion is every bit as hereditary as their hairline. In other places, a loathsome distortion of Christianity—such as a prosperity gospel or a liberation theology—is so widespread that its acceptance has eclipsed that of the truth it impersonates. Many places in Latin America, Europe and Africa fall into these categories. Some in these groups profess to know Christ, yet they don't know His gospel. For example, in much of Latin America faithful Catholics will insist that they believe in Jesus as much as anyone. But it's what they don't know or believe about Him—his unique mediation between God and man, His wholly satisfactory work of atonement on our behalf, His call to repent and trust solely in Him for salvation—that compels us to take the gospel to them.

This is where a survey of churches is particularly useful. How in the world do we begin to determine what "believing in Christ" means to the people in a certain locale? Generally speaking, a look at the churches will suffice. Churches have statements of faith, public services and (usually) trained ministers, all of which help make the theological persuasion of a congregation sufficiently transparent. Those professing belief in Christ who place their membership there are unlikely to have a personal statement of faith highly at variance with the creed embraced by the congregation. Therefore, it seems wise to acquaint ourselves with the number of believers who attend gospel-preaching churches. A disciple maker surveying the need in a city cannot count the thousands in churches that may be preaching a false gospel as "reached" people. For instance, in China, sadly, many of the gains for Christianity so celebrated in the West have been made by some churches that are entirely divorced from the gospel. The unbelievers who fill those pews need to be made into disciples of Christ just as much as their Buddhist neighbors.

On the other hand, there are some places in the world where gospel-preaching churches are a common sight. I grew up in one such place, a town in Ohio of about fifty thousand inhabitants. As I am not acquainted with the state of every church in my hometown, I can only affirm that there are multiple dozens of churches that, lesser theological distinctions notwithstanding, faithfully proclaim the gospel to unbelievers. Adding together the memberships of these churches would provide one with a rough idea of the progress the Word has made in my hometown, and thus of the level of need for Great Commission disciple making.

Of course, in a place like Ohio there are many people who have not joined themselves to a gospel-preaching church who nevertheless are quite familiar with the claims of Christianity. Which brings us once again to the *unheard* factor. Say that the total number of congregants at gospel-preaching churches in my hometown is fifty thousand. Does this mean that the Great Commission delineates a "need factor" of thirty-five thousand? Once again, I don't think so. The Great Commission doesn't tell us what to do with people who reject the good news we preach, but the book of Acts gives us some idea of how Paul viewed this problem. Paul's short stays in small towns indicate that he was not primarily concerned with repeating the gospel to the same group of unbelievers over and over, year after year (e.g., see Acts 14:21-23). Of course, in every place he went where people believed his message and trusted Christ, a church—usually comprised of but a handful of disciples—was left in his wake to be that faithful outpost of gospel proclamation. Nonetheless, Paul's departure clearly shows that he saw the need as lying elsewhere.

The *unheard* factor means that each of us must consider where we can go to be an agent of disciple making among those who have not heard the message. Maintaining that there are some *unheards* still in your city is insufficient—what is your plan for finding them and engaging them with the gospel? If the *unheards* are so few that you don't how to find them, or if they are greatly outnumbered by the number of believers who could give them the gospel, it's time to consider a needier place. In no way am I suggesting that every Christian should pack up and leave town (more on that later). It just seems to be reasonable that if there are five Christians for every *unheard* in a given place, many should.

In summary, when we consider the need in any place (whether the "where" we are now or the "where" we aspire to go), the Great Commission leads us to this type of inquiry. What is the disciple-making workload of the believers already here? What percentage of the professing Christians are likely to be true believers, based on the creeds of the churches they've joined? Are there enough *unheards* to keep all the believers here busy proclaiming the gospel?

Finding the Clots

This leads us, then, to consider the world. Questions like those we just discussed work like a medical dye-contrast test, causing certain regions to leap off the map at us and demanding that we wrestle with entering into disciple-making efforts there. As Christians with the mission settled in our heart, can we be unmoved by the condition of places like Saudi Arabia, whose population is more than 95 percent Muslim? Can we fail to even consider the disciple making we might do in the spiritual darkness of northern India? Can we flippantly reassure ourselves that there's work to be done at home, just as much as there is in the metropolises of China?

Then there are other regions on the map, highlighted by the Great Commission, that we may not be accustomed to thinking of as needy of the gospel. Some of the major cities in Christianized nations may not feel much like mission fields when compared to a malaria-ridden African village, but they are nevertheless chock-full of *unheards*, a situation aggravated by a severe shortage of gospel-preaching churches. Likewise there are places in the world that are now considered by many to be passé mission fields (e.g., Latin America, the Han Chinese) that are drawn back into our consideration of the need by these questions.

A comparison of the places that are highlighted by these questions presents us with a corresponding set of challenges. Once we've caused the neediest places to rise to the surface, we're in a position to ask what similarities—besides their spiritual neediness—these places have. If a doctor sees several patients with similar symptoms who all work in the same building, he's going to suspect an environmental cause. Why are these people sick while others are not? Analyzing the unbelieving population of the world will have a similar effect: we will notice that certain types of places tend to have a high degree of neediness. This discovery is of great strategic value, as it helps us to identify and prioritize those places in the world where the *unheard* factor is high. It also helps us to make a wise plan to make disciples in that kind of environment. We begin to see that in order to make an impact in those places where the *unheard* factor is highest, we must prepare ourselves to face some enormous challenges.

1. The Challenge of Cities

Once we've determined that we're looking for places where there are many unbelieving individuals, the dense urban centers of the world grow prominent on our radar. If the Great Commission sends us to those places where *unheards* abound and churches are in scarce supply, then big cities are clearly delineated as the most needy places in the world. This is not to deny that people in rural areas need to be reached; rather, it is to say that there are by definition more people who need to be reached in the city. The Commission does cause us to consider where we will have the opportunity to engage the most *unheards*.

Though some people may buy into the stereotype of the missionary living in a jungle among half-naked cannibals, this is far from the truth. There is an overwhelming need for a new generation of missionaries sent forth to target the explosive growth of the world's urban centers. In China, where we work, for instance, people are pouring into the cities from the countryside. The city of five million or so where we live is in the process of building a new district that will hold tens of thousands of households. Such urban growth is typical not only of China, but of the developing world in general, especially in those places that fit our criteria of need outlined above.

So what is needed? A kind of missionary who can become an urbanite, dealing with the stress and risks that city life brings, and welcoming the opportunity to immerse him-or herself in city streets teeming with millions who have never heard the gospel. This context virtually guarantees a lifetime supply of potential disciples from among the world's *unheards*.

2. The Challenge of Closed Countries

Further comparison of the needy places in the world will reveal that a very large portion of them are located in closed countries. Though the term *closed country* is considered as outdated as anything I've said in this chapter, the label is still useful for describing a place where missionaries are not welcome. It is certainly not to say that a missionary cannot go, but only that a missionary will not be welcomed as a missionary by the governing authorities there.

It is important to understand that the type and severity of persecution that believers face is not identical across these many nations. The suffering that Christians are subjected to may range from social exclusion and restrictions on congregating to brutal arrests and criminal courts. For example, the Chinese government generally is very slow to take action against house churches and uses virtually no measures to restrict personal conversion, but they actively oppose house churches that grow too large or act too publicly. However, in many Muslim countries, even conversion is illegal, and proselytizing can meet with severe repercussions. Regardless of the restrictions of the government, God's kingdom mandate overrules and impels us to go and make disciples for as long as we can.

So what is needed to meet the challenge of closed countries? It is common to think the answer to that question is "cleverness"—a creativity that births novel schemes for staying in a country that wants missionaries out. Thus, missionaries to closed countries often teach English, open coffee shops or start businesses. However, the examples of missionary work left to us in the book of Acts lead us to a different answer: boldness. What is needed in China, Morocco and Uzbekistan is not clever ways to stay, but courageous ways to go. What we want is not creativity, but courage in proclaiming the gospel. If we are booted out of one place, there are many more places on our map of neediness where we can work.

3. The Challenge of Culturally-Distant Contexts

Another look at the places that stand in great need of Great Commission labor shows that many of them are in cultural environments vastly different from those to which Westerners are accustomed. The gap between you and these *unheards* is far more than just geographic. It is also linguistic. I, for one, believe that the Chinese language is just as large an impediment to the work of disciple making here as are any of the Communist government's restrictions. The gap is also seen in these societies' lifestyle, their cuisine, their customs and their homes. Even things like the climate, the healthcare and the traffic in a region compound the difficulty of an outsider's attempts to plant himself there.

So what is needed of would-be goers? Simply put, they must be willing to endure hardship like soldiers. We've probably all seen pictures of American soldiers in the Middle East and marveled at the miseries of heat they endure while sporting head-to-toe gear. Our Lord's command must give us something of the same power to adapt and endure. We are under orders too! Out of a deep desire to magnify the One who called us, a believer finds the grit to bear up against the most adverse conditions, learning seemingly impossible languages, eating unfamiliar foods and going without some creature comforts.

A Good Place to Start

These are some of the great challenges of our missiological moment, of our time on the Great Commission's front lines. Reaching most of the *unheards* in the world will require tackling of these challenges. While it is of course true that there are also *unheards* in places that don't fit these descriptions, this is where the vast majority are to be found. This means that a modern believer must think it likely that he or she likely belongs in a place like this!

A couple more thoughts on the subject of need and then we'll move on. First, it is never necessary for us to resolve to find the neediest place in the world. Why? Imagine I showed you a set of buckets filled to various levels with water. Then I gave you a single cup of water and told you that my goal was for all the buckets to be filled to the top. Could that information alone tell you which bucket to pour your cup of water into? I haven't told you to pour your water into the bucket with the lowest level of water, though that would certainly be in line with the goal. As long as the water from your cup goes toward filling up the buckets, you are meeting the need.

The Great Commission informs us that Jesus wants the gospel message to fill up the world until no *unheards* are remaining. There are many "right" places to pour out the meager offering of our lives, places where the need is far greater than I know how to meet. For instance, I live in a city of millions of *unheards* that continues to grow every year. The size of the bucket terrifies me, and there are hundreds of places in even greater need around the world. This doesn't mean that I need to leave where I am to go there, only that I must be willing to go if someday the supply of *unheards* in this city dwindles in comparison to the number of believers here. If I have more water in my cup than the bucket has space for, I best be looking for a new place to pour!

That is exactly the kind of place that many Western believers call home. True, there are some *unheards* in most every town. But if the bucket is close to full (there are few *unheards* remaining), and there are hundreds and hundreds of other Christians preserving their cups of water, just waiting for an opportunity to give the gospel to *unheards*, is it not self-evident that there are many infinitely more useful places you could go dump your little cup of water? Ten thousand Christians could pour out their lives in Indonesia, and the bucket would likely remain unfilled!

We must also realize that many believers will not choose to order their lives by the Great Commission. Which means that it's long past time for Christians who feel the Commission's weight to stop saying things like, "Well, we can't all go to the mission field." We are so far from that extreme, the very suggestion that this is a danger we are likely to face is laughable. The church, with its current distribution of Christians, is like a boat with ninety-five people sitting on one end and only five sitting on the other. The side with ninety-five is sinking and the side with five is raised ridiculously out of the water, but no one moves. "We can't all sit on that end," say the ninety-five. No, but twenty or so would be a good start!

May God grant that one day our churches do in fact wrestle with the question of how many they can possibly send while still maintaining an equally vibrant witness to their own community! But in the boat we're in now, it would be a good idea for a missions-minded believer to start asking the following questions:

- *Where can I go where others will not?*

- *Where can I go where others have not?*

- *Where can I go where others could not?*

Questions like these are sure to lead you to a place of great need where you can worshipfully and usefully pour out your life.

5

Questions of Gift

Are some people more uniquely suited for this work than others?

Many believers feel the same way about the Great Commission as I feel about jazz music. I intellectually understand something about the objective value of jazz, and I certainly bear no grudge against the genre. I'm not trying to wage a one-man war against the saxophone, but it's just not for me. It's not a good fit, you might say. My musical appreciation lies in other, admittedly less sophisticated places. Jazz just makes me uncomfortable. On many a jazz-filled elevator ride, I have found myself making awkward eye contact with the other passengers. "Are we supposed to be dancing right now? I really hope not." I think many believers have heard about the need for missionaries and have felt a similar discomfort. "Sure, missions is all well and good if that's what you're called to do. But it just doesn't sound like my thing."

To put it another way, there are many Christians who really don't have many questions in the areas of duty or need, but hesitate to make a move towards reaching *unheards* because of questions of gift. They grasp—at least partially—that there are places in the world that are in desperate need of the gospel.

Neither is Christ's command to make disciples actually very difficult for them to accept. But when you talk about picking up their lives and moving to places of great need, they can only respond that they don't think it would be a good fit for them. They feel their gifting lies in other areas.

Unqualified Disciple Makers

I must say that it excites me to take a few pages to talk about this particular perspective on the Great Commission. Because in my experience, it is the response that I most often encounter when discussing the needs of missions with those I perceive to be the greatest candidates for this kind of work, i.e., college students and young couples. When talking to young couples faithfully serving in churches back home or when talking with college students sincerely desirous of building God's kingdom, the most common thing I hear from them is, "I love missions and disciple making, but I just don't think I would make a good missionary."

I am usually convinced of the integrity of this answer. It is, after all, based on a good premise. That is, there are obviously going to be some people who ought to remain right where they are, trying to reach all remaining *unheards* in their community and serving as a repeating witness to all unbelievers, even though there are much needier places in the world. It is further assumed that those people who remain for what might be called *home missions* or *domestic disciple making* should be uniquely equipped for that task in the same way as those who go as foreign missionaries are uniquely gifted for their work. Many Christians then, after taking stock of their gifts, declare themselves to be better suited for ministry at home. Others have a more pessimistic view of their own abilities, and simply doubt that they possess any of those traits that would make them good candidates for foreign missions.

My hope for this chapter is to demonstrate both to the self-professed "nongifted" and the "differently-gifted" that the factors that fit you for foreign missions are likely not what you think. I pray my "differently-gifted" friends will discover their giftedness to not be a hindrance to their going as missionaries, but an impetus. And I pray my "nongifted" brothers and sisters will find that they are already qualified in the most important ways for involvement in worldwide disciple making.

Not Going Doesn't Mean Not Going

While the Bible makes clear that there is a wide range of giftings that a Christian may possess, it is important for us to remember that the purpose behind them is but one. No gift is an end in itself, but all gifts exist that the church may effectively pursue its Christ-appointed goals. This means that disciple making is no more a gift than worship or the edification of fellow believers. Can you imagine a Christian who didn't come to church services because he didn't believe he possessed the gift of corporate worship? Or a Christian who neglected the Scriptures because she claimed to lack the gift of studiousness? These activities are essential parts of living as God's people; the various abilities that God gives us, on the other hand, serve to empower us each to contribute individually and vitally to these goals. So some of us may make more dynamic progress in the study and interpretation of Scripture, but that doesn't mean that the rest of us find another book to read!

What does this mean for us as we consider how our own gifting relates to the goal of disciple making? It means that regardless of our current geographic location, we are all to be busy about the work of reaching the *unheards*. If you remember, this is what we said the word "go" implies in the Great Commission: an unceasing quest to discover and make disciples out of unbelievers. So even those Christians who ultimately decide to stay where they are must do so with the unreached in mind.

I think this is clear to most missions-minded believers. I only pause here momentarily to define terms. Because really we're talking about "go" in two different senses. One is the "go" we just mentioned—continually moving proactively towards unbelievers. The second is the one that causes all the fuss—this "go" refers to changing geographical locations in order to bring the gospel to those without it. It might be helpful to think of this "go" as "exportation." You may truly "go" in the first sense without being "exported." A Christian who finds himself in a community with large numbers of *unheards* may be "going" in the first sense (as he intentionally engages and shares the gospel with unbelievers), even though he stays right where he is! Exportation, however, occurs when a Christian decides to "go" in the second sense (leave town) so that he can "go" in the first sense (preach).

The issue that specifically needs to be addressed in light of our questions about gifting is: aren't some people gifted in an unusual way to "go" in the second sense? Meaning, granted that all Christians are expected to be "going" to make disciples (first sense), isn't there still room to say that not all Christians are equally qualified to be exported (second sense) disciple makers? Again, I believe the answer is yes, but I want us to think carefully about just what those unique qualifications are! As we said at the start, many are of the opinion that they haven't got those qualifications.

So far, we've said the issue must not be "Who is going to make disciples and who isn't?", but "Who is going to be exported to make disciples and who isn't?" With that in mind, let's look at two kinds of reasons to not be an exported disciple maker. Two ways to stay, you might say.

Staying For Now

In Acts 13, we read of the ignominious false start of Mark's missionary career. Upon Barnabas and Paul's original deputation by the church at Antioch, they appoint Mark to go as an assisting member of their team (see Acts 13:1-5). After the first short leg of that first missionary journey, however, Mark bails on them (see 13:13). We're not told whether there was a specific difficulty that Mark was unprepared to face. For example, if Cretan food didn't agree with him, or if he just missed his mom. One thing is clear: Paul isn't happy about it. The next time Paul and Barnabas decide to put together a missionary team, there is serious argument about whether or not Mark has any business on a journey of this kind (see 15:36-40).

Paul and Barnabas's disagreement supports our original premise, that there are in fact certain people who should remain where they are. The reason Paul wants Mark to stay—and the first reason many modern Christians should stay put—is that he is not ready to be exported. In other words, some believers have no business attempting to go to other locations to make disciples, because they lack the characteristics that would make them effective disciple makers in that context.

What is included in this lack of readiness? Mark's story implies that it includes what some might call character flaws, but what we as believers might more appropriately think of as missing structural components in our sanctification. Most any missionary can recount in painful detail the ways in which moving to another cultural context puts intense pressure on the foundations of your heart and causes ruptures at points you thought had long since been stabilized.

Service as an exported disciple maker definitely requires a measure of independence, as you are often in places where few people are your spiritual elders. If you're lazy or undisciplined, unwilling to learn or unable to put up with discomfort, removing the supports of your present church family may plunge you into depths of uselessness that you've never before plumbed. We must not forget that the goal is to make disciples ("go" in the first sense), not to change zip codes ("go" in the second sense). If you're likely to pull a Mark, it would be wise to not go. Sadly, probably every missionary with a few years of experience has witnessed his fair share of abortive missionary careers that were the result of a believer being launched out into the mission field without adequate preparation.

The thing to remember about this first reason to stay is that, in most cases, it describes a changeable condition. Not just a condition that can be changed, but a condition that the gospel demands we change! The steady, renovating power of God at work in a believer's sanctification will inspect more and more of the cracks, fissures and bows in our hearts, and shore them up through deeper faith in Christ. While all of us are at various points along that lifelong process of renovation, there are some whose hearts are still in such a state of disrepair that they can't bear the pressures of exportation. Even though the structurally-suspect nature of an immature believer's faith ought to preclude him from the pressures of being exported, his goal (as well as the goal of his church) should be to one day be "exportable." For this reason, we can say that the first way to stay is to "stay for now." Although Paul would rather go without Barnabas than with Mark for now, one day he will call Mark a profitable member of his missionary team! So while I readily concede that this is a valid reason to stay put, it is not a valid reason to stay put forever!

Obviously there are many mature Christians who also struggle with questions of gift. When they say they don't think missions is the right fit for them, they don't mean that they consider themselves too spiritually immature to handle it. They are saying something quite different. Let's look at the second way to stay to see what they mean.

Staying For Good

Very rarely do you meet a person (though they're lots of fun when you do!) who has so deeply confounded the two senses of "go" that they truly believe that the primary characteristic of a missionary life is mobility. That is, they think that what really makes someone a missionary is their inability to stay put! They dash tirelessly and frantically from one place to another trying to reach some *unheards* here, some unbelievers there. Most would agree this thrashing, this refusal to settle in a place, is more of a testimony to a short attention span than to a commitment to the Great Commission. The glory of missions is not in the luggage or ticket stubs, but in the nitty-gritty process of disciple making. That process only happens when you stay, not when you leave.

Every Christian should be willing to leave where they are, but every Christian must also be willing to stop somewhere, sometime. I agree fully, as I tried to say in an earlier chapter, that a mission-minded believer must not lay deep roots, and that every one of us must be willing to leave if that is what Christ's command leads us to do. But even as a missionary exported to China, I am considerably stationary. The most effective disciple makers that I've met, and probably that you've met, are quite settled in a certain locale. Why? Though we must always be willing to go again, all of us must stop "for good." "For good," not just planting yourself in a certain spot for the foreseeable future, but "for good," as in choosing a certain spot that will allow you to benefit many people.

Let's repeat and rephrase a little. This second way to stay says, "It is expedient for me to remain here, for in this place I am of maximum use to the work of making disciples of the world's unbelievers." It stays "for good" for the good work of proclaiming the gospel to unbelievers and training disciples to obey all that Christ commanded. This is a Christian who has considered other places and has concluded that there is more than enough work to do where he is right now or that he would be more useful to the cause of Christ here than elsewhere. This second way to stay is where we all ought to end up, but that doesn't mean it will look the same for all of us.

Not long ago, a recent college grad and I were in a friendly debate about some of the issues discussed in these chapters. He mentioned a well-known pastor and author in the United States whose ministry has been blessed with immense influence and a wide audience, and asked me if I thought that this pastor was wrong for staying in a relatively Christianized part of the world—an excellent point. It seems clear that there are certain individuals who are unusually effective in the work of disciple making right where they currently are, and, as was just stated above, it is wise for every believer to consider where they would be the most effective disciple maker. I think this famous preacher shows one of the possible ways to "stay for good". He has chosen to remain in a place with comparatively few *unheards*, and yet he has been used to edify millions from his pulpit. His unusual

effectiveness is precisely what should lead us to advise most believers to decide to "stay for good" in a different way.

Why? As I told my just-graduated buddy, you're probably
not that well-known pastor! It is extremely unlikely that you are
one of the rare breed whose gifts make them highly effective in
an environment with few *unheards*. I understand that I, for one,
have far more meager abilities, and I have found that my feeble
attempts at gospel preaching and disciple making make a much
larger difference in northeast China than they likely would in the
northeast United States! While I am extremely thankful for the
ministry of men like him who are unusually gifted, it is unwise
for young believers (particularly his admiring seminarians) to try
to duplicate his ministry. You're probably not him. You'd likely
have far more opportunities for disciple making in another place
where the gospel is in greater scarcity. It must also be pointed out
that no one knows the kind of impact that well-known pastor
would have made if he had gone to Laos!

I visited a church plant not long ago in a growing American
city. The strategy for the plant was well-researched, the leadership
team was highly talented and organized, and the service was
God-honoring. They had done their homework and it showed.
And yet it seemed the dream just wasn't becoming a reality. Years
into the plant now, they've barely got a core—and very few
new disciples at that. Please don't do these guys the disservice
of imagining that they're not gifted enough or called enough
or passionate enough. We're told by people who research such
things that the vast majority of new church plants in America
fail. When I see church planters in those guys' shoes, I want to
beg them to come to China. It's not that people in China are
so much more open—it's that such a larger part of them have
never heard, and there's a much smaller number of men and

churches striving to reach them! Before you protest that there are many places in America in need of church planters (which is true), there are about a dozen other church plants in these guys' backyards, in addition to the dozens of established churches in the community. These wonderful brothers decided to "stay for good"—but I fear that there may have been a much greater good they could have done elsewhere.

Another group of people who may decide to "stay for good" is older believers (not necessarily old, just not as young as they used to be!). With their best language-learning years behind them, and with a limited time before them to prepare for foreign missions, many older believers wisely decide to stop where they are to work towards the same goal of worldwide disciple making. Not long ago I was talking to a doctor whose lifestyle and generosity have testified to his love of missions. Entering the second half of his career, he was taking stock of his Great Commission effectiveness and wondering if he should do something extreme, like give up his medical practice and become a missionary. While I'm all for doing extreme things, I was happy that our ensuing brainstorming session turned toward the prospects of his doing more in disciple making locally. At this stage in the game, it would be unlikely that he would readily learn a new language or undergo intensive missionary training. But what if he used his remaining disciple-making years to train five younger men, some of whom would become disciple-making missionaries in other countries? That would unquestionably be a decision to "stay for good!"

In summary, "staying for now" means that you are currently in no condition to be exported, although one day you will be. "Staying for good," on the other hand, means that you have chosen to get off the exportation train at a strategic location, and that you will remain there until you are providentially moved, no longer effective, or dead! It is considering where in this world you can do the most Great Commission good.

Get Burdened

Now, some people can get as far as this but still have some serious questions of gift, specifically about their personal burden and skill set. Let's talk about the burden first. It is common to hear young believers say something like, "I just don't have a particular burden for taking the gospel to another country. Don't get me wrong. I love missions, but I'm more burdened about something else."

Burdened is a slippery word, but I get what they mean. It isn't keeping them awake at night, like maybe some other things are. It isn't what they're dreaming about. It doesn't weigh heavy on their hearts, filling their prayers with pleas on behalf of the world's *unheards*. They are hardly alone. In fact, most Christians don't become missionaries, not because they've made a careful decision to "stay for good," but simply because they don't feel any special way about missions.

So what can you do if you're in this boat, besides give yourself up as uncalled? First of all, it's hard for me to believe that any believer with the Holy Spirit producing fruit in his life feels absolutely nothing about the lost condition of unbelievers around the world. Burning jealousy for God's glory, aching compassion for condemned sinners and zealous ambition for Christ's command, but never frigid indifference, are the things that must fill a believer's heart when he or she thinks of the world. So maybe a better way to express this apparent lack of burden is to emphasize the *particular* part. Many believers don't feel *particularly* burdened for reaching *unheards*, or they don't feel as strongly about giving the gospel to millions of unbelievers in another country as they do about giving it to the dozens they know in their hometown.

So, then, we must acknowledge that believers never have just one desire. There is never a single burden that fills our hearts. We are always stirring up certain desires and suppressing others. We choose to live each day in the light of particular burdens and to relegate others to the background. When two conflicting desires crowd into our view, every one of us prioritizes, choosing to encourage one and thus adding fuel to its flame.

We must further acknowledge that there are some desires that we should feel more keenly than we do. Whether from long disuse, or from an inappropriate fueling of a competing desire, there are some burdens that aren't particularly strong only because we haven't strengthened them, and not because God doesn't intend for us to feel them strongly. This is why the heading of this section is *Get Burdened*. We normally think of a burden or a desire as something that just comes upon us without rhyme or reason, and we are simply acted upon by those desires which rise to the surface from the murky depths of our hearts. But there are so many commands in the Bible for us to feel certain ways and desire certain things that it becomes abundantly clear: we are responsible for stirring up certain emotions and burdens (see Luke 10:20; 1 Cor. 12:31; 1 Pet. 3:14; 1 John 2:15).

Is the desire to bring the gospel to the world's *unheards* one of those that we must stir up? Given both that it is a command of our Lord Jesus Christ to us, and that God our Father himself feels strongly about the unbelieving world being called to worship before Him (He did send His Son to die to that end), most believers would answer with a resounding "yes!" So when you discover that you have no particular burden for the millions of *unheards* the world over, you must not conclude that you must not be called. Instead it's time to realize the gap between your feelings and God's, and then get about the business of stirring up some of your burdens that have been languishing.

How are we to go about strengthening these malnourished desires for evangelizing the world's unreached? I don't want to go into this question too exhaustively here as it will feature prominently in the next chapter, but for now let's affirm that all of the desires God wants us to have are provoked and elicited by looking into the truth. In other words, all that God wants us to feel is true, and any deviation from those feelings is due to our buying into deception and falsehood (see Matt. 13:44; John 17:17; Col. 1:9-12; James 1:22-24). So when a Christian doesn't feel about the unbelieving world the way God does, it's because his view has been skewed in some way. Which truths, specifically, will help us feel about the world the way God does? We'll save that for later.

One further note, though, about seeing the way God does. In discussing these matters with believers, it has been surprising how often I'll run into someone who wants to stay put in order to reach a few particular individuals in his or her life. They say it would feel hypocritical to go to the end of the world with the gospel if they haven't even given the gospel to these dear friends. I couldn't agree more. So get a plan for sharing the gospel with them! Five or ten individuals for whom you are especially burdened do not constitute a five to ten year plan! For a Christian to make several unbelievers for whom he is strongly burdened the whole of his attempts to disciple is just another way to have his burdens out of line with the truth. To pass up opportunities to bring the gospel to many more because of your burden for a few is ultimately like trying to play God—electing whom you will and passing over others!

Get Skilled

As we said at the start, it's common to hear believers who do feel burdened about missions protest that they are not qualified to be missionaries themselves. Many of the same things can be said here as were said above about burdens. While I completely agree that those who are gifted should be exported as missionaries, there is a great deal of misconception concerning what those gifts actually are. Consider for a moment the following possibilities.

First, you might not even know what skills are going to be needed. I have had more than one young man who were truly passionate, effective disciple makers tell me that they shouldn't be missionaries because they wouldn't make good pastors. I have always been very happy to inform them that not every believer who goes as a missionary (even a church-planting missionary) must serve in a pastoral role! Besides that, it was very obvious that their idea of pastoral ministry was heavily influenced by some of the extrabiblical baggage that has been heaped upon the office over the years. They loved to make disciples, but thought they would hate the role of a pastor or missionary! A tragic misconception if there ever was one! We must not mistake the external circumstances of missionary life (language learning, traveling, support raising, cultural adaptation, etc.) for the essence of missionary work. Those other things are just trappings. The essence of the missionary commitment is making disciple making among *unheards* the central focus of your life's work!

Second, keep in mind that you just may be a lousy judge of missionary qualifications! If you've never moved to another country, learned a language, adapted to a culture, witnessed to Hindus, or trained a pastor, you might want to ask someone who has before you declare positively that you could never do any of those things! You may not be able to imagine yourself as a missionary, but that might just mean you have a sorry imagination! It might be a question best left to others (more on that at the end of the chapter).

Third, don't underestimate the effects of good training. One of the aforementioned young guys who didn't want to serve as a pastor had just earned his degree in business. He explained to me how he wasn't gifted or skilled in the areas full-time ministry required. Funny that he had never considered that the only reason he knew anything about business was that he had spent four years studying it in college! He has never proven that he's skilled in business—he just feels like he knows what he's doing because he has received training! Frankly, it's a little unfair to say what you could never do when you've never undergone preparation for it! Many of the most effective missionaries I know spent years in intensive training before being exported! Why not try to get some training as if you were going to be a missionary, and then ask other people if they think you're exportable or not?

Fourth, remember that, like the desires of your heart, your talents and abilities are not singular, nor are they set in stone. If you are convinced that the Great Commission is to be your ministry paradigm, you must diligently emphasize and cultivate those abilities you have that are most likely to make you an effective disciple maker. In other words, you will choose to make some of your skills side acts and some to be the main event. The

Great Commission paradigm helps us choose which ones to put where. You may be a wonderful dancer, great with numbers, top of your marine biology class or an Xbox master. But, without denigrating any of these good gifts, having a skill is not necessarily a reason to prioritize it and place it center stage in your life. A huge number of Christians who think themselves unqualified to be exported have stuffed some key disciple-making abilities into some hall closet with their golf clubs, and might become valuable additions to a missionary team if only they were to dust them off (the abilities, not the golf clubs)!

So please don't prematurely close the door to being an exported disciple maker. Don't insist that you don't have the necessary qualifications. Because skills, like burdens (and probably an affinity for jazz music, for that matter), can be acquired.

Suspect Your Motives

In conversing with young believers still calculating their future course, I have found that for the most part they are far too trusting of their own motives. For example, I have met some guys who have told me that the part they see themselves playing in the Great Commission is remaining in their home country, making as much money as possible, and giving generously to the efforts of gospel proclamation worldwide. Do you see the irony in that? Let me quickly affirm that I am in favor of radical generosity, but even the briefest of acquaintances with the human heart surely causes us to be suspicious of such altruistic statements. If you are one of those sincere people who think this way, don't you think your motives are even the teensiest bit suspect? Anyone, believer or unbeliever, would happily accept the role of millionaire philanthropist! You must at least suspect that such a decision is based more on your unexamined desire for the security and comfort of wealth, and intuitive repulsion at a missionary's vagabond lifestyle, than on a careful weighing of your potential contributions to the Great Commission!

Ironically, one of these would-be givers told me in the course of conversation that he suspected his motives for wanting to be a missionary! While a determination to examine his motives is praiseworthy, he has failed to expose his other aspirations to the same exacting X-ray. Some may protest that all of our motives in serving God are at best mingled with selfishness, sloth and covetousness. But that is all the more reason for us to default to the work most clearly indicated by the Commission rather than speculate about our potential usefulness in rare capacities. If God has commanded us to move toward the world's *unheards*, you need to work on the right motives to go—but you need to go! I am quite positive that many days my motives for staying in northeast China are absolutely vile; but I'm not sure that I'd do much better on a plane home, either.

Briefly, here are two additional asides to these sincere brothers and sisters. First, most of the people I hear saying this have not proven that they have an unusual ability to make money. It's godly to give money if you have it (see 1 Tim. 6:17-19). It's not godly (or wise) to make money your lifetime pursuit, even if your intention is to give it away (see 6:9-10). Second, the greatest obstacle to the advance of missions worldwide is not financial. Believe it or not, man power is needed far more than money power.

Don't exempt any of your ambitions from the process of examination. What are the reasons that you think you should be one of those who stay behind to reach a few, rather than one of those who are exported to reach many? Can't you hear how suspicious those reasons sound?

The Church of Volunteers

I know, I know. We can't expect everyone to be exported, or who would be left at home? But look for a second at the application lines. The huge majority of believers you know are filing their proverbial paperwork to get permanent residency right where they are (or in an environment similar to it). Meanwhile, the number of people in the "exportation" line are mighty few. We are so far away from anything resembling balance in this regard that, as I noted earlier, it is silly to be talking of the danger of sending too many! That's why I would encourage every reader to simply volunteer to go to a place of challenging need. Maybe you'll end up being unqualified; but there's no harm in volunteering, is there—unless you're afraid of someone calling your bluff.

Imagine a church where all the leaders, all the staff and all the maturing disciples of Christ had publicly made known their desire to be exported wherever the church believed they would be useful. Imagine, then, that church training all its members and striving to make them exportable. This church would find itself ideally suited to make strategic advances towards the world's unreached. They would be free to select those whom they believed to be most qualified and export them to needy places around the world.

Now it's unlikely you go to a church like that. My point is only that volunteering is a step in the right direction for all believers. The more volunteers a church has, the better. Every last one of us must be willing to go anywhere to allow our ambitions, dreams and plans to be swallowed up by the wartime concerns with which the Great Commission confronts us. But how can we bring ourselves to volunteer? The next chapter will try to answer that question.

6

Questions of Cost

What is a Christian's motivation in Great Commission work?

When the excuses for not moving towards worldwide disciple making are stripped away, most believers usually react in one of two ways. The first is relief: a deep sense of liberation. There are some missions-minded believers out there who would genuinely love to give their lives to Great Commission work, but have felt like they were unqualified, uncalled or unneeded. Helping them resolve some of their questions about duty, need and gift is like throwing open the gate in front of a racehorse. They blast off toward the world (usually with their overseeing leadership begging them to slow down a bit and get some training). Others, however, have a drastically different reaction—terror. To them, it feels more like the fence between them and the Grand Canyon's edge disappeared into thin air! They stagger back, horrified, from the chasm that has suddenly opened before them! It turns out that while their reasons for staying put sounded legitimate, their petrified reaction to the undoing of those reasons reveals that they weren't as willing to go as they led others (and maybe themselves) to believe. Those reasons were only excuses brushed with a thin coat of logic.

What Are You Afraid Of?

What is the source of the fear that causes believers to shrink back from the call to go to a needy place? What is it that drives us back from the edge? If my own bouts with fear are any indication, it's because we realize the potentially devastating cost of missions. You might say we get a bad case of spiritual sticker shock. Over and over, I've seen students and young couples come to the very brink of the yawning abyss of need only to turn away shaken. They see their duty; they see the need; they see their giftedness; and they are repelled finally by the price they may have to pay. The questions of cost, unlike the previous ones we've discussed, are rarely vocalized. They are whispered fearfully to our will from the most secret part of our heart. We see what's required and tremble. So what's down in that dark canyon that causes us to lose our nerve?

The unknown, for starters. Volunteering for exportation to a needy place somewhere else in the world means that you are agreeing to morph your life into something almost unrecognizable to you now. It means exchanging the apparent security of sticking to the well-worn path before you for a treacherous trail winding down into the darkness below. What will your life be like ten years from today? If you're committed to following the trail of *unheards* wherever it leads you, it's hard to be sure where you'll be living, what language you'll be speaking or with whom you'll be working. No one likes to be out of control of their life, and to many the fear is overwhelming enough to turn them back.

Then there's the threat to our own plans. Especially for those college students and newlyweds who have carefully thought-out plans for their lives, the idea of being exported to another place as a missionary has all the appeal of a dentist's chair. The most talented and ambitious young people rarely turn their attention to the unheards of Algeria or Pakistan—they've already got a plan, and that clearly isn't it. For them, volunteering would potentially cost them their dreams, aspirations and goals. I can identify with this a little, I think. When first directly confronted with the Commission's demands on my life, I already had some fairly crystallized plans for my future. There was no mistaking it. I was at a clear (and terrifying) fork in the road. The needs of missions fit into my plans like a bowling ball fits into a neat arrangement of pins.

There's discomfort down in that canyon, too. It's a near certainty that exportation will very often be an unpleasant experience. There are harsh climates and unpalatable cuisines. There are impenetrable cultures and incomprehensible languages. There's brutal learning and demanding work—not to mention the deep disappointments and heart-wrenching agonies of suffering. And then, of course, there are all the things that there's not. There aren't grandparents for your kids, nor are there friends you grew up with. There's often not adequate healthcare or safe streets. Making disciples in Southeast Asia or West Africa would certainly not be a very dull life, but there are far less agonizing ways to get an adrenaline high!

These are just a few of the monsters lurking in the darkness below. There are still the fears of persecution, of failure or inadequacy, of being unknown or forgotten, of financial insecurity and many more. To really persuade you to buy into becoming an exported missionary, now might be a good time to tell you that there are ways around all of these costs, that we can go in and talk to the manager and he'll knock some money off the ticket price; but that can't be done. There is no avoiding it. To live a life driven by the directives of the Great Commission is to open yourself up to painful loss. So it's best not to deny it in the first place. There's a good chance that it will even cost more than you can now imagine. I could introduce you to missionaries who have been arrested, who've contracted life-threatening illnesses, who've been beaten, whose daughters have been raped, who've been held up at gunpoint and whose houses have been robbed. It's a wonder anyone becomes a missionary when you consider how much there is to lose!

But I hope in the rest of this chapter to share two main thoughts with you. First, there is a way that we can stand on the brink of this abyss without wavering. That is, we can prepare our hearts to pay whatever cost is necessary to bring the gospel to the world's *unheards*. Second, there is a glory in the cost so great that someday we won't want to go back and remove the cost even if we could! We will ultimately discover that the cost is part of the way that God shows himself glorious through the disciple maker's life.

Eyes on the Prize

The Summer Olympic Games are going on as I write this, and as always, they are a marvel of athleticism. Every event features incredible men and women doing something that I feel sure I could never do! Whether they're swimmers, runners, gymnasts or cyclists, they all seem to be born to compete in their respective events. But it would be insulting to those athletes to suppose that they're at the Olympics just because of good genes. Though many of them have without a doubt inherited an unusual set of physical attributes and abilities, that's at most only half the story. The other half is thousands of hours of grueling training—a staggering cost, in other words. What do you think is the average cost of an Olympic medal in terms of time, money, strained relationships, aching muscles, lost sleep, skipped desserts and raw emotions? Put it like that, and it's easy to see why most people will never be Olympians.

So what is it that drives that incredible level of discipline and sacrifice in great athletes? I don't think that's difficult for any of us to understand. They run for the prize. Every sacrifice they've ever made has been a declaration of the value of the prize. To practice halfheartedly, to skip a training session, to cheat on their diet or to quit and go back to a regular life would be to deny its worthiness—to admit that the goal isn't really worth all the trouble it brings them. But because they value so supremely the medal they pursue, they pursue it at all costs.

The same determination is discernible in the testimony of the apostle Paul. At the end of his life, Paul says that he has finished the great race and fought the good fight (see 2 Tim. 4:7). This is his way of referring to the work that has eaten up his best years, heaped heartache upon him, gotten him tortured cruelly and landed him on death row! It's an unusual way to describe a fight in any case, but especially one that ends like this! What rejoices his heart in this cell? He tells us in the next verse that all that's left for him to do is to receive a crown. We'll talk about what that reward actually is in a minute, but realize first that in these final miserable days of his life, the thing he's thinking about is the prize, not the pain.

To finally confirm in our minds that this is what lies behind the believer's ability to suffer loss in obedience, we need look no further than the example of Christ himself (see 1 Pet. 2:21). Jesus endured the cross and despised the shame thereof, not because he superhumanly didn't mind pain or humiliation, but because his heart was in pursuit of the glorious joy on the other side of the tomb (see Heb. 12:1-2). When we are most tempted to tap out of our own race of obedient faith, it is this patient endurance of Christ that we must ponder, and in which we must hope (see 12:3). Jesus ran to the pain of the cross with his gaze fixed on the joy of his coming exaltation to the glorious right hand of the Father (see John 12:23). The only way we can run to obey the Lord's commands—including his Great Commission—is if our gazes are similarly fixed on future joy set before us!

So it seems safe to acknowledge that the key to our ability to pay an overwhelming cost is to see through the loss to the surpassing value of what we pursue. If there is any doubt about that, we will be sure to shrink back from our duty and the world's need. Those believers who have serious questions of cost have filled their hearts with the realities of suffering, discomfort and insecurity. As a result, they will forever be stuck on the lip of this precipice unless the glorious joys of the Great Commission shine brightly out of that canyon before them and allure them down the road of sacrifice.

In the last chapter we said it was encountering the truth that would allow us to change the contours of our heart's desires. This is exactly what we mean here as well. Until the prize is as vivid and visible to our hearts as the misery of sacrifice, we will never go all in. As long as the pain of being separated by thousands of miles from your family is more vivid than the joys of being exported as a missionary, the sacrifice will never be made. While the fears of the unknown life that awaits you in North Africa are crystal clear, and the glories of proclaiming the Gospel to Muslims are at best murky, you will put your wallet away and continue looking for a less costly life.

Joy, the Powerful Motivator

It's not hard to get people to feel sympathy, or even pity, for missionaries. In fact, a large amount of financial giving is drummed up by appeals to these sorts of feelings. While pity for missionaries may propel the financial engine of missions, this approach rarely results in an increase in Great Commission manpower. Why? Because sympathy and pity are heartfelt appreciations for the pain of another. We could say they are "pricetag-focused." Based on what we just said about cost, we can't expect young people to start volunteering for exportation until the glories of worldwide disciple making are exalted higher than all the "occupational hazards" of missions. This is one of the reasons I am opposed to the kind of missionary reports that seem primarily intent on arousing pity for the hardships and deprivations experienced on the field. As long as believers in less needy places are trained to focus on the cost of going to needier places rather than on the glories of doing so, we can expect very little overall movement according with the Great Commission's directions.

There's another deficient motivation that doesn't result in effective exportation of believers. Those with a desire to be mobilizers for missions often appeal to guilt and shame to cajole believers into going to the world's *unheards*. How lazy and ungrateful must we be, they ask, to sit comfortably at home while the world burns? While there is no question that sloth, among other things, is an enemy to the cause of missions, this type of browbeating is unlikely to result in self-sacrificing commitment to the Great Commission.

When I was a kid enduring the rigors of swimming lessons, there was nothing I feared like the diving board. But since my friends were actually brave enough to do so, I would succumb to peer pressure and line up behind them to dive. Looking down from the dizzying height that ten feet is to an adolescent, I wanted to retreat back down the ladder so badly, but shame always won out. Over and over again, I would hurl my fear-paralyzed body down into the deep end of the pool with a painful flop. While it seems like the shame of being wimpier than my friends was an effective motivator to get me to jump, guilt and shame never provide the power to thrive and persevere. As my notable absence from the Olympic Games confirms, I never amounted to anything as a diver. Eventually I learned not to go up the ladder in the first place. We may be able to guilt some people into doing a bit more for missions today, but we won't guilt them into becoming faithful disciple makers who remain despite the escalating costs.

All this is to say that we must realize the joys of missions if we are going to proceed. It is the only kind of motivator that will build a disciple maker willing to be exported anywhere. Until we see how incredibly gracious God is to allow us to participate in his work of worldwide redemption, we will never dive in. So, with all this in mind, I can think of no better place to turn in this chapter than to the glorious joys of being an exported missionary. If we see missions as terrifying and not electrifying, it's because our hearts are not filled with these truths. No amount of arm twisting will get you off the diving board if you don't see that joy. Once you do, no one can hold you back. What are these great joys, testified to by almost two millennia of Christian missionaries? What is the prize on which their gaze has been fixed through every imaginable horror and loss? Most basically, what's so great about being exported?

1. The Joy of Glorifying God

Thanks to the faithful teaching ministry of several authors and preachers over the past several decades, this foundational motivation for missions has been implanted into the hearts of a generation of disciple makers. I've been privileged to meet missionaries to some of the most challenging fields in the modern world who are driven by the chance to bring glory to the name of God. They joyfully put everything on the line that God may be shown to the unreached peoples in all his magnificence. In order to put us all on the same page, let's take a few moments to review just how it is that preaching the gospel to the *unheards* worldwide brings glory to God, and how that in turn gives us joy.

Sin is depicted in the Bible as fundamentally being a refusal to worship God. Though mankind has known God, in the sense of knowing He exists, every person has failed to make God . . . God! In other words, they've failed to treat God the way that God deserves to be treated, i.e., worshiped. But man is a worshiper without an off switch—there is no stopping his honoring, praising, sacrificing and obeying of *something*. So whenever men have turned from God, they have not become atheists in the strictest sense. Instead, they have directed the endless outpouring of their worship to things which are not God, but impostor gods, called idols. Thus, man was plunged into a blinded, God-less night (see Rom. 1:18-25).

Enter the promises of God. God chooses Abraham and swears that through him, all the earth will be blessed, implying that the world will one day return to the worship of the God they've spurned (see Gen. 12:1-3). Then, throughout the history of Abraham and his descendants, we find God again and again acting in a way that demonstrates the greatness of His power, wisdom, mercy and justice not just to this one family he has chosen, but to peoples all around them (see Gen. 41:38; Exod. 11:9; 1 Sam. 17:47; 1 Kings 10:9). The ignored God acts famously. But none of these mighty manifestations culminate in the kind of worldwide worship the promise led us to expect. Furthermore, the prophets continue to allude to a future time when the whole world will be filled with the glory of God (see Ps. 72:19; Hab. 2:14).

Enter the sum and climax of God's promises, His incarnated Son, Jesus Christ. He was the ultimate revelation of God's glory (see John 1:14; 14:9). And via His atoning work, believers were and are restored into a right relationship with God, whereby they live to honor and glorify Him in all that they do (see Rom.15:8-9; 1 Cor. 6:20; 10:31; 1 Pet. 4:16). Paul tells us that in the gospel, the glory of God was made visible to believers through the work of Jesus Christ (see 2 Cor. 4:4-6). So when Jesus commands His disciples to take the gospel into all the world, we hear him saying that the time the prophets spoke of is already upon us (see Luke 10:24; Acts 13:38-48). We are God's agents of glorification in this world. By the message we declare, we call the multitudes to see the glory of God in the work of Christ. We are working toward God's goal of making His greatness known on a worldwide scale, that none of His creation would remain in the darkness, but that His glory would shine into every corner.

This is an endless source of joy for an exported disciple-maker. When I look around this Chinese city and see how unknown God is here, just how few ripples the knowledge of His magnificent existence makes in the fabric of this society, I must grieve that God's worship is plundered daily. But when I am unspeakably privileged to proclaim the name of Christ here, I must rejoice, for I am helping to make Him famous! This endeavor is so gigantic that its gravitational pull lures all believers into its orbit. It dwarfs the cost! To increase the knowledge of God on the earth is to multiply the most valuable capital that exists. Nothing I can sacrifice is to be compared to it. If you're stuck on the diving board, this is a beautiful joy that beckons you to leap!

2. The Joy of Obeying Christ

Many of the great missionaries in the church's history have been motivated by the simplicity of obedience. The fact that Christ has commanded the thing to be done is reason enough to give up great possessions, great expectations and great ambitions and humble oneself to bear the cost of the Great Commission.

Paul spoke several times about his ministry as a task entrusted to him by Christ. His was to be a pioneering work that would lead to Christianity's expansion among the Gentiles. For example, in his farewell discourse to the Ephesian elders, he admitted that the Spirit had made clear to him that great afflictions awaited him when he arrived in Jerusalem (see Acts 20:22-23). But this was no reason, in his eyes, to change his plans! He happily gave his life in order to complete the ministry of gospel proclamation that was entrusted to him (see 20:24). God had given him a work to do, and he valued obedience more than the cost.

Earlier in the record of Acts, when forbidden to preach any longer in the name of Christ, Peter and John respond that obedience to God must take precedence over any man's command (see 4:19-20). The advance of the gospel to the world was not repelled by man's threat. Again we see that the desire to obey Christ is far stronger than their desire to avoid the cost (suffering). They had been commanded to be witnesses, and disregard for Christ's command was simply unacceptable.

But what makes obedience a gloriously joyful thing? The postmodern bent of western culture tells us the opposite—that submission to authority is a threat to our freedom and therefore to our joy. But ask a soldier if there's joy in obeying orders. Ask an obedient child if it makes her miserable to submit to her parents. I am not denying that there are times when submission is noxious to everyone. But aren't there times when we willingly follow orders and find in our hearts a definite accompanying satisfaction? Why is that? I think the answer lies somewhere in our inner senses of purpose and mission.

Have you ever heard someone say something like, "I was meant to do this" or "I was made for this"? To what are the people who utter these grandiose words usually referring? Are they talking about some bit of dullness or drudgery in their lives that they can't seem to escape (as in, "I was made to file income taxes!")? Or are they exulting in some task that gives them such joy and is the very reason they get out of bed in the morning? In other words, having a sense of purpose is linked fundamentally to joy. Purposelessness is almost a synonym for depression. When we sense that we are doing something that meshes seamlessly with our very being, the resulting emotion is joy! This isn't the joy that comes from self-determination, but the joy that comes from submission to a higher will.

Now, when we hear a voice of authority giving us a command, we can either recoil in distaste, rejecting its intentions for us (and thus choosing to look for joy elsewhere), or we can embrace it happily, accepting its purpose as best for us. To obey, then, is to accept and pursue the purposes of another. If that purpose, then, is one of those that are fundamentally aligned with our being, we can expect joy to result from that obedience.

And when that authoritative command is from the God who created our being, we can be sure that the purpose His command proposes to us is precisely what fits us—the mission for which we're on the earth. When a Christian obeys the command to take the gospel to the *unheards*, he can sense in his heart that he is doing just what he was meant to do. There may be immense costs to exporting your family to Central Asia, but you can face the discomforts and challenges that each day brings with the joy of knowing that you are fulfilling your God-given purpose. You are doing just what He made you to do.

3. The Joy of Redemptive Ministry

Compassion is another powerful motivation for missions. Seeing the truth of the world's deadened condition before God must stir in our hearts the same longing that Christ felt. Over and over we are told in the gospel accounts that Jesus was deeply touched with compassion for the unbelieving people around Him. Though the multitudes were fully deserving of His righteous judgment, He loved them and longed to restore them into fellowship with Himself. Observing the accursed nature of this sin-riddled world must wrench our hearts in the same way. We, as His body, cannot be unmoved by the masses of people who are without hope and without God. Rather, our hearts must ache deeply for the plight into which sin has borne them. But compassion, in spite of how often we have seen it used this way, is not supposed to lead us into the dead end of helplessness and guilt. God has granted that we should be part of His redemptive activity, bringing these soon-to-perish *unheards* back to Himself. God doesn't just want us to hear cries of help in a burning building; He has given us ladders and hoses to rescue the perishing.

If you ask many veteran missionaries what their greatest joy has been, some of the other joys mentioned here may make an appearance, but this is the one most likely to spring to the front of their minds. When the gospel message we proclaim comes within the hearing of unbelievers, the effects are potentially explosive. Those who give their lives to making disciples of the *unheards* become witnesses to the unbelievable things that happen when the life-giving Word is set loose in a dark place.

I am fortunate enough to be part of a closely-knit team of a couple dozen missionaries serving all over the world. Every couple of weeks or so, we like to give each other some brief updates, sharing some needs and developments in our ministries. The encouragement that I reap from that single thread of e-mails is truly empowering. Hearing about those who had been dead in their trespasses and sins in South Africa or Chile and have now been saved by God's grace never fails to bring me new energy for the work in China. This joy of lost souls passing from death to life is felt all the way to God's throne, and it adds gas to the tank of any disciple maker.

This is what Paul tells us in Second Corinthians 3. He tells the Corinthians that if anyone should be sure of his status as a minister of the gospel, it is the Corinthians. They're the last people that would need to check Paul's references. They themselves are Paul's resume, the proof of his ministry. How so? Paul says that they are like a letter written with the Spirit of God on tablets of the heart. He's saying that the Holy Spirit has conducted a transformative, life-giving work within them. They were dead, but when they encountered Paul's preaching of the gospel, new life appeared! Paul says that this is the glory of our ministry. Others may doubt the value of Paul's work, but he couldn't possibly begin to doubt it himself. He had seen the dead come to life!

This is the testimony of missionaries the world over, from ages past to the present day. Read the words of John Paton, the nineteenth century Scottish missionary among the cannibals of the New Hebrides Islands, as he describes the first time his fledgling church plant took Communion together. "For three years we had toiled and prayed and taught for this. At the moment when I put the bread and wine into those dark hands, once stained with the blood of cannibalism, but now stretched out to receive and partake the emblems and seals of the Redeemer's love, I had a foretaste of the joy of Glory that well-nigh broke my heart to pieces. I shall never taste a deeper bliss till I gaze on the glorified face of Jesus Himself."[19]

An exported disciple maker has more cause to rejoice in the discovery of new life springing into existence under his preaching than a biologist discovering a new species, an astronomer discovering a new star or an explorer discovering a new continent. Not only because this new life we see birthed is superior to all those other discoveries, but also because we humbly realize that God has allowed us in all of our insufficiency to be the planters of that life-giving seed. Our missionary career in China has still not stretched as long as many, but I can testify that this glorious joy has helped establish us here. We, too, have seen the dead come to life—a sight well worth the cost!

Reflecting on that same Communion Day, John Paton wrote further, "My heart was so full of joy that I could do little else but weep. Oh, I wonder, I wonder, when I see so many good ministers at home, crowding each other and treading on each other's heels, whether they would not part with all their home privileges, and go out to the heathen world and reap a joy like this—'the joy of the Lord.'"

4. The Joy of Magnifying Christ's Atonement

But what if we go to a place where the *unheards* don't respond? This is truly a fear for many teetering on the edge of commitment to missions. It would be wonderful to see lives changed, but there are some fields where men have faithfully proclaimed the gospel to an ever-increasing number of *unheards* only to be met with rejection time after time. Where is the joy in that? Where is the joy in what many would call failure?

When I think about this question, I am reminded of Paul's joy in Second Corinthians 2. In an outburst of praise, Paul gives thanks to God for always causing him to be victorious in his gospel-preaching ministry (see 2 Cor. 2:14). This seems almost ironic in the context of Second Corinthians, where the apostle seems rather rocked and embattled (see 4:8-12). Not to mention his impressive catalogue of suffering that he logs later in this book! (see 11:23-28) So how does Paul keep a straight face and tell us that he never loses? He goes on and tells us that through the work of his team's gospel preaching efforts, the aroma of knowing Christ is spread everywhere they go (see 2:14). Paul obviously can't mean that people respond positively to the gospel wherever he goes. Acts tells us that they don't. Also, he plainly tells us here that they don't. In the next verse, Paul tells us that there are actually two ways to perceive this fragrance (see 2:15). To those who believe, the aroma is life-giving. Those who respond in faith to the gospel receive new life. But to those who don't, the aroma is the stench of death (see 2:16). To those who reject the gospel, it is a message of utter condemnation. But remember what Paul has said—he personally always wins (see 2:14)! Meaning, there is no scenario where we lose when we spread the fragrance of the gospel, regardless of whether or not people reject it.

How can this be? Imagine that a king has just soundly defeated an insurrection. A part of his kingdom has rebelled against him, and he has crushed it. Then he sends his heralds to all the places he rules, broadcasting the defeat of his enemies and warning all rebel sympathizers to give up the cause. His loyal heralds love the king and are ecstatic over his victory. But many of the people in places to which they will travel have no such sentiments. In some of the town squares where they proclaim the news, they meet with angry glares, cursing, threats and violence. What joy is there to the herald in that moment? It's still the king's victory! He still rejoices that the king has won. His enemies may rage, but they will not win. To the herald, there are only two unacceptable possibilities: that those loyal to the king would mourn, or that those rebellious against the king would rejoice! And the news he bears disallows both those possibilities. These enemies of the king may have rejoiced the day before his news, but they will not rejoice today! The king's victory has been proclaimed, and for that his heralds are happy!

I think this is similar to Paul's declaration of his perpetual victory. Though the message of the gospel is loathsome to some, a messenger of the gospel can't lose because each and every proclamation of the gospel shows the glory of God's grace, mercy and justice. When people repent at our preaching, we marvel at God's mercy shown to rebellious sinners. But when people's hearts harden at our preaching, we marvel at God's holy and omnipotent justice in His defeat of sin. Of course this rejoicing in God's justice is mingled with a sober sorrow at the fate of souls precious in God's eyes and our eyes alike. But this sorrow does not take away from the preacher's victory! He was commissioned to bear the message, and he has faithfully, passionately done so. He has released the fragrance and allowed it to permeate this place. To some it brings life; to some it brings death: but the objectively glorious value of the aroma never diminishes in one iota. The only unacceptable scenario is that the aroma is contained, its beauty bottled up and unknown to the world.

A host of Christian missionaries over the centuries have felt compelled to go to the world's unreached chiefly because of the extravagant love that was shown to them personally through the cross. As an expression of thankfulness and deep happiness in the work of Christ, they have offered their lives to spread the aroma around the world. It has simply seemed logical to them. What Christ has done is so overwhelmingly good that they can't help but magnify His goodness the world round. Whether or not their audience perceives it as good can't undo the joy that they feel in their regenerated hearts. For those of us who tremble in fear of rejection, it would do us good to look long at the cross until we feel that same compelling joy.

5. The Joy of Divine Commendation

Rewards get a bad rap. Many Christians rightly feel distrustful of superfluous talk about our receiving rewards. After all, there seem to be much loftier motivating forces available to the servant of God, and the idea of doing something to get rewarded seems base, and more self-gratifying than God-focused. Nevertheless, the biblical authors repeatedly encourage their audiences to consider the prize that awaits those who persevere in obedience to Christ (see Matt. 5:12; 2 Tim. 4:8; Rev. 22:12). This doesn't necessarily mean that our prize-seeking motives in preaching the gospel are greedy or selfish. Though cutthroat businessmen, bank robbers and doping athletes also are all motivated by prizes, the fact that God instructs us to seek prizes implies that, in those other cases, something has gone wrong with a basically good motivation. So what exactly has gone wrong? What's the difference between a Christian's joy in reward and a fallen, broken prize-seeking behavior? The answer is certainly multifaceted, but let's try to look at one key aspect of this difference.

Despite my best efforts in a number of pursuits, I never got a trophy for anything when I was a kid. It is a deep shame that still pains me to confess. Now that I'm older and wiser, I understand that trophies have no inherent magical properties. Nor are they necessarily objectively valuable; they come from a store, not the US Treasury! Although I wanted a trophy so badly as a kid, I have never been seriously tempted in adulthood to go have my own custom-made! Even though I could afford to get one that would have been the envy of all my junior high friends, somehow I know it wouldn't be the same. You could pay to build a replica Heisman trophy for yourself, but you would never look at it in the same way as a football player who actually won the real Heisman. It turns out that who gives the trophy is pretty important to the joy that we get out of it. The trophy is but a physical manifestation of the approval and recognition from the one who awards it.

This is why Paul doesn't just say that he's anticipating a crown. Instead he says he's awaiting a crown of righteousness from the righteous Judge (see 2 Tim. 4:8). That is, the crown comes from Christ and is representative of his just commendation. The bent and distorted prize-seeking behavior that characterizes unregenerate man continually confounds the value of the reward with the value of the rewarder. It thinks it can attain the joy of approval without conforming to regulations, failing to realize that the greatest part of the happiness resulting from a prize is knowing that it is given righteously, justly. And what makes the rewards from God's hands unique is that no one will ever get a reward from Him unjustly—you may cheat the Olympic committee, but you will never cheat God. So any reward that comes from Him should be a source of glorious joy.

This probably is part of the reason why Scripture is surprisingly sparing with details about the rewards we will be given for faithful obedience. Most agree that the multiple references to crowns are probably meant to cause the original audiences to think of the athletic competitions so familiar to their culture, not to lead us to believe that we will each have a personal stockpile of bejeweled headgear. In spite of quite diligent and wrong-headed attempts by some teachers to find one, there is no outline in the Bible of a hierarchy of reward levels. When Peter seems to wonder what he and his fellow apostles will receive for abandoning all to follow him, Jesus doesn't roll back curtain number three! Instead He just says, in essence, "infinitely more" (see Luke 18:28-30). The emphasis of the Bible remains on the reward of divine commendation. The joy of hearing God formally announce His approval of our labors for him is the great reward Paul and all who obey faithfully rejoice in (see Matt. 25:21). Paul says the crown he's awaiting is given to all those who long to see Christ (see 2 Tim. 4:8). Simply put, take Jesus away and there is no reward.

So back to the joy of exported disciple makers. What thrills the hearts of missionaries who pay hefty prices to bring the gospel to the world's *unheards*? The knowledge that their labors do not go unnoticed, and will one day meet with the public approval of the One they love. You there, teetering on the edge of missions, need never fear that your work in a slum somewhere in India will be "unrewarding." For one of God's children, it will be the most deeply rewarding experience that your unexported self can now imagine: a life met with our Father's commendation. This joy of reward can never be severed from joy in God Himself, but neither can our joy in God be separated from our desire to live lives that meet with His approval. With Christ strengthening us, we can.

6. The Joy of Eternally Significant Work

Missions, as a category, merges all too easily in the mind of many Christians with the category of vacations. There seems to be some overlap between them that explains the confusion. Many people *doing* missions take short trips to exotic destinations, much like vacationers. The result of this misunderstanding is that there will probably always be a certain sort of Christian who feels attracted to missions in the same way he or she is attracted to beaches, amusement parks and ancient ruins. It seems enchanting, thrilling and refreshing. Many short-term trips that churches make only reinforce this confusion by majoring in fun and minoring in, well, missions. Some believers even become full-time missionaries while still laboring under this delusion! The only sure cure I am aware of for this misunderstanding is long-term missions! There's nothing quite like a year or so away from home in a developing nation to effectively rub off all the sparkle from our enchanting mission field dream. Sooner or later you discover the awful truth: preaching the gospel to the world is work.

And to some, that's the end of it. If it's work, then there's no joy to be had in it. Work is what we go back to when joyous times are over. To someone who is accustomed to living for the weekend, missions has little appeal. When you rest from your labors in China, there is no football; there are no bass boats and no steakhouses. So to the work-despiser, there's little draw to become an exported missionary.

To others this news is just as much of a downer, though in another way. These people have the much more biblical understanding of work as a fundamentally good, pre-Fall institution of God (see Gen. 2:2, 15). God works, and His created image-bearers ought to work, too (see 1 Thess. 4:11). They know that God is glorified by a Christian who does his work as unto the Lord, and not unto men (see Col. 3:23), but they already have picked out a job that they're thrilled about doing, and the idea of proclaiming the gospel worldwide as work puts it in competition with that beloved occupation. If it was something like a vacation, they might be able to accept it. To make it a career, however, is asking too much. So to the work-lover, missions also seems a bit much.

In the end, the work-despiser and the work-lover are both stuck on the diving board—and they will be until they see the joy of Great Commission work. Why does worldwide disciple making bring joy as labor in and of itself? Because of its deep intrinsic importance. As we have already seen, exported disciple-makers stand in pivotal places for the advance of the gospel. The news of Christ's offer for forgiveness of sins and eternal life is in their hearts. Thus, the rising sea of God's worldwide plan that spans millennia now sends its waves lapping onto the shore I stand on in northeast China. When this ocean of eternal import is felt at your back, the result will be a humble joy in your work role.

The work-despisers need to feel that they were built to work. You may have always felt that work was a dry, insipid thing to be endured. You may have felt that work was just the way to get money to pay for fun toys. But when you see God's purposes in our work, you can rejoice in the seemingly mundane aches and sweats it brings. The grander that purpose, the happier and humbler we will feel. When the missionary inevitably finds himself investing long hours into the spiritual growth of national believers, he rejoices to know that his work is so important that God is his coworker!

The work-lovers need to sense that there may be work even more valuable and necessary than the work they love now. It is tempting to believe that you could never be happy doing anything else, but don't underestimate the joy that comes from embarking on a mission of eternal scope and import. In this regard, the consistent testimony of countless missionaries in many times and places tells us that exported disciple makers can rejoice in the process—in the very work itself—of missions, not just in the results.

Not Exclusive, but Driving

Lest I be misunderstood because of my exultation in the missionary's work, let me make clear that I know that these joys are also at work in the lives of those disciples who remain unexported. If you work as an elementary school teacher in the southeastern United States, I hope you are motivated by these kinds of joy-giving truths, too. My purpose for writing this, then, is not to show that these joys are exclusive to missionaries. Rather, it is to show that joy alone will enable a missionary to count the cost and go forward anyway. (I don't believe God would call you away from the career you have or pursue because you lack these joys, but rather on the basis of the questions discussed in previous chapters!) For those who fear missions and shrink back from the call to make disciples of the nations, overwhelming joy is required. This chapter is written primarily for those who have peered into the darkness and shuddered, doubting whether joy could really survive down in that pit. It can.

It's hard to focus the attention of our hearts on many different truths simultaneously, so it might be worth taking a final moment to ask how these joys relate to each other. Is there a way to think of them together? What would it look like if a person was perfectly driven by all of these joys at the same time—completely committed to glorifying God and obeying God, showing compassion towards sinners, magnifying God's saving works, pursuing divine commendation and doing eternally significant work? Well, it would look a lot like Jesus! As we saw in our look at Hebrews before, Jesus is our model in motivation. What drove Him in His atoning work for us is the prototype for what will drive us in our proclamation of that work.

At the risk of oversimplifying, the answer to our motivational dilemma is the gospel. We will only take the plunge off the diving board when we see that Jesus took the greatest plunge already for us. Do you fear the cost? Do you tremble when you think of encountering what's down that dark path that leads to the world's unreached? Read some missionary biographies and see that they, too, trembled.[20] Then see the joy that drove those disciple makers to take that path. Look deep into the joy that the gospel brings . . . and leap!

7

Making a Shift in Emphasis

How high of a priority do our churches place on the Great Commission?

Hopefully the past chapters have helped to stir up some serious consideration of our Lord's Commission and what it means for us personally as believers. In this next section, I want to trace out some of the major ways that Christ's mandate to reach the unreached applies to the emphases we make corporately as His body. In other words, as churches all around the world, what are the implications of the Great Commission for how we think about and do ministry? It's hard for a list of implications to be exhaustive, so I'm going to limit myself to four areas where it seems our emphasis must undergo a shift—but shift we must. It is essential for us to begin to see all we do in the ministry of the church through the lens of the Commission.

Everyone Wants a Slice

Every local church has a set of emphases. They can also be thought of as priorities. An emphasis is any area where the church commits a significant portion of their resources, such as their manpower, their teaching time, their budget, their planning, or their staffing. If, for example, your church has an emphasis on enriching the community, it is by allotting a segment of this pool of resources that the change in the community will be effected. Plans are made, money is set aside, programs are created, responsibility is delegated, volunteers are recruited and sermons are given, all with the intention of pushing the church's members toward impacting their community. We could say that the bigger the slice of the total resource pie that goes to a given endeavor, the larger the emphasis.

Now, most churches have at least a slice of the pie designated for the worldwide propagation of the gospel. This slice is inappropriately small in the vast majority of cases. Though our thoughts may fly immediately to our churches' financial commitments, let me reiterate that that is only one ingredient baked into the pie. As I said earlier, finances are currently not the greatest hang-up in missions. Let's think of our churches as a whole—all we possess and all we do—and measure what portion of that total resource pool is directed to the work of worldwide disciple making.

Let me be clear: I am not saying that the whole pie should go to the world's *unheards*. I'm only saying that more should go. It might be helpful if we think of the pie pieces in kinds or categories. Again, following Wayne Grudem's simple outline of the church's purposes, there are three basic ministries our congregations must not neglect: their ministry towards God (worship), their ministry towards believers (nurturing edification), and their ministry towards the world (proclaiming the gospel, or engaging *unheards*).[21] I think most pastors would agree that those three purposes could effectively sum up all that they want their own church to do. All the pieces of the church's resource pie should end up doing one of these three things. If so, we can color in this pie chart using just three colors: one for worship, one for edification and one for worldwide disciple making. What I will insist about missions, I would say just as doggedly about the other two pieces. We must not permit any one of these three things to be swallowed up by the other two. They are all purposes of the body of Christ on the earth, and if we discover one of them to be underdeveloped or withering, we must rush to breathe some life into it.

Making the Cut

Those of us who have been given charge of a local congregation of believers must consider carefully in what directions we are herding our flocks. We lead them into the presence of God for worship and repentance. We lead them into community with each other for admonition and exhortation. We also lead them to engage the world's *unheards* for bold proclamation and testimony to the gospel. If we are not intentional in any one of these areas, we should not expect our churches to become centers of worship, Bible teaching or disciple making.

But how large a part of our resources should be given to our ministry to the world's *unheards*? I imagine that an evangelical church which truly didn't emphasize the mission at all would be rare indeed. Few of us are struggling with whether or not to prioritize the Great Commission. For the most part, we're all doing something and wondering if it's enough. As the need of the world would dwarf the abilities of any one congregation, no matter how large, need alone cannot serve as an indicator of the sufficiency of our efforts. There will always be more *unheards* than my church can reach, even if we gave the whole pie to the effort! So just as each church has to make crucial decisions concerning how best to lead its congregants into worshiping

God and building up their faith, the plan for involvement in worldwide disciple making is also a matter for each of our local churches to sort out for themselves.

Again, part of our mission to the world involves maintaining a witness in our own locale capable of continually filling our cities with gospel teaching (see Acts 5:28). So we can't even say that all of our evangelism resources will go to other places. In some cities, a church's evangelism resources won't begin to fill up the need in their immediate area, so it is appropriate that a majority of these resources be used to target the many *unheards* around them. But for those churches that find themselves in an area that has few remaining *unheards*, the Great Commission demands that those resources be channeled into more unreached places. Workers, dollars, projects, teaching and leadership need to start flowing toward the ends of the earth. Regardless of how far away from our church's geographic location our evangelistic resources are being used, whether among illegal immigrants in our own city or among the academic elite of a Chinese city, we want to be sure that they are used primarily to reach those who have not yet heard the gospel.

Measuring Emphasis

So is there a priority being placed upon worldwide disciple making in your church? After all your pie pieces have been accounted for, what is your church's net contribution to the work of gospel exportation? Here are some questions to ask about our churches that might help reveal blockages in the pipes that carry resources to the unreached:

- *How many missionaries have been sent out of our church?*

- *How many members of our church have visited a mission field?*

- *Is there a clear strategy outlining our church's mission efforts?*

- *How many students have expressed interest in missions service?*

- *Are members volunteering themselves to be exported?*

- *What percentage of our church's missions giving goes to* unheards*?*

- *How does missions giving compare to our church's total budget?*

- *How often is the need of the world's* unheards *publicly taught?*

- *Have remaining unreached segments of our own city been identified?*

- *Is there a plan in place for reaching our own city repeatedly?*

The point of these questions isn't to put any of us on a guilt trip. I have little doubt that in most of our churches, if these questions have less than encouraging answers, it's because a strong emphasis has been placed on other worthy, God-honoring things. Hopefully these questions show us that, in many cases, one of the three central purposes for the church may be suffering from a lack of attention and resources. As we saw in the last chapter, ultimately this means that the church will be cheated out of a measure of the joy that God has intended for it to possess as its members live in obedience to Him. So it's time for us to sit down and think about how we as churches can allocate our resources to cut down the world's *unheard* factor.

Thus, in each of the following chapters, we will examine one of the emphases common to modern churches, then talk about how it is turned on its head by the push of the Great Commission. When we start to make decisions with the world's *unheards* at heart, in which new directions will our resources flow? Of course, unless you find yourself in the very unusual position of having more resources at your church than you know how to handle, considering new emphases for your congregation means reallocation of resources away from other things. It means using your precious preaching time to teach more on missions and thus less on something else. It means sending your teens on more missions trips and thus on fewer other kinds of excursions. It means giving more money to further the gospel's advance and thus less to use in other places. Since this tension definitely exists for most of us, the following chapters are also geared to talk about some things from which we must consider taking resources. This may not go over very well, but something always has to get cut. I'm not sure we can wisely allow these other emphases to take precedence over the Great Commission.

Corporate Benefits of Personal Emphasis

Regardless of how certain you feel that your own role in the Great Commission is not as an exported missionary, it is still vital that you personally exhibit a radical commitment to emphasizing world missions. Why? Because a missionary does not spontaneously spring into existence in an emphasis vacuum. At some point along the pathway of this missionary's life, he was taught to prioritize worldwide disciple making. There were others in his life who exhibited passion for God's worldwide fame, compassion for fallen man and obedience to the Lord's command. He saw brothers and sisters in Christ who prioritized the Great Commission with every resource at their disposal, and that triggered in his own heart a similar burden to order his life according to the demands of the mission. In short, he became a missionary because of the emphasis of others.

I often have people ask me how in the world I ended up in the frozen extremities of northeast China. The answer is fairly disappointing for a lot of people, I think. The fact is, my role as a church planter here is nothing more than the result of God's gracious work within me through the influence of a few men who were radically committed to the Great Commission. I was but dry wood that got too close to their fire. With friends like these, it's hard for me to imagine having ended up anywhere else! Let me briefly introduce you to a few of those men. I wouldn't take the time to do so unless I was pretty sure that (1) most missionaries who have been exported around the world have also been deeply impacted by the emphases other men have made; and (2) most maturing believers relate to at least a few people in some of the same ways that my influences related to me, and therefore you are in the same strategic position to influence others.

My Pastor

I grew up in a church that emphasized missions to an unusual degree. It was a larger church, but its financial giving to missions was out of proportion to its size. Missionaries were in our church almost weekly, sharing reports of their work in countries all over the world. This prioritization of the Great Commission was far from accidental; it was the unswerving focus of our pastor. My pastor never went a whole service without reminding the church of our worldwide calling. He personally visited missionaries a couple times a year and became deeply invested in several works in particular. He was the one who took me on my first missions trip (to the Philippines) when I was a senior in high school. He had a little meeting with me and explained why he wanted me to go with him. Besides my wife and I, several other families have been sent out of this midwestern church in recent years. Why? Relentless emphasis on the Great Commission by an un exported, impassioned pastor over the course of a generation.

My Friend

Then there was the longtime friend and coworker who I told you about in earlier chapters. He was a couple years older than I was, so he had graduated and gone off to a Bible college by the time I was giving serious thought to ministry. But he never failed to look me up when he was back home from school. He would give me books about missions, recorded sermons about missions, tell me stories about missions. He basically unloaded about missions nonstop until he went back to school! As I said, he took me to go hear a missionary speaker who knocked my worldview for a loop—and he still didn't let up. He could tell that though I expressed a burden for missions, I had very little chance of actually ending up exported. So he pushed me to get training with a veteran missionary in Peru. Sensing my tendency towards life-wasting far more acutely than I did at that time, he all but pleaded with me to go, saying that he would even pay for my plane ticket. Now a missionary in Morocco, this brother, just a hair over thirty, has been used to propel men on three different continents to give their lives toward propagating the gospel. His work in Morocco is one not only of evangelism, but of exportation—training new believers in a Muslim country to give their lives (maybe literally, if the threats they receive are any indication) to magnify the name of Christ where most fear to speak it aloud. What is it that has made my friend such a catalyst for corporate movement (not just his own) towards the world's unreached? A passion that has resulted in a rare set of priorities; a life with an emphasis stubbornly placed.

My Mentor

Finally, there is that veteran missionary who has been a mentor to me for eight years now. When I got to Peru, I soon discovered that what I thought was a reasonable amount of passion for the Great Commission looked like indifference when compared with this old dude's! Not only did I witness the continuing growth of a church-planting movement in that city, I got to look under the hood at what was turning the wheels. A formidable force of Peruvian preachers of the gospel were swarming all over the city and chomping at the bit to go to the unreached around the world. That fire had been fueled for many years already by the time I arrived. Feeding that native fire was this American missionary, with a house full of maps and globes over which he prayed constantly, a copy of *Operation World* never out of reach, and a regular schedule of long powwows about missions until late hours with whoever cared to listen. And many of us did care to listen!

As I said earlier, I am privileged to be a member of an incredible team of disciple makers, all of whom were raised up around this missionary's commitment to the Great Commission. Wherever this man has gone, he has, by the priority of his own life decisions, challenged young men to give their lives for the unreached. I, for one, was swept up by that steady fervor for God's worldwide fame. I caught the passion more than I was taught it. He was the one who first accompanied me to this unknown corner of the world's most populous nation. It was His plan, His dream, His desire to plant churches here that was transplanted into my own heart. His unyielding emphasis on movement towards the unreached eventually bore fruit in my life.

So you can probably see why I am happy to admit that I am the product of my influences. My own movement to the world's *unheards* was due more to the passionate priorities of other men than to the uprightness of my heart. Seeing the good guiding hand of God operating through the brightly burning emphasis of others, I am all the more intent on being the same kind of force for young believers in this Chinese city. I want to display a radical commitment that draws attention to God's worldwide work to such an extent that others are swept up into the flow of my meager resources as they move toward the *unheards*. Any single disciple maker can only be exported to one place at a time, but by placing an extraordinary emphasis on the unreached, the current of our lives can break up some of the sediment holding others back from flowing on to the world. So I say, even if you believe you should be one of the unexported, or even if you have already been exported to a place with a high *unheard* factor, this does not exempt you from emphasizing the Great Commission for the sake of other believers.

I could tell you many more stories of men I have met who have, from within their individual callings and paths, emphasized Christ's mandate with their every resource, and in so doing have lit many other fires with their scattering sparks. Businessmen who gave extravagantly, pastors who preached intentionally, parents who prayed diligently and professors who instructed passionately—all by their commitment to world missions challenging others in the body of Christ to give their all. So no matter who you are or where you are heading, don't think for a second that this talk of a corporate emphasis on missions is of little significance for you. Put your emphasis where it belongs, and you may start to see a movement toward the world from among those closest to you.

A Model of Radical Missions Commitment

In order to illustrate the kind of emphasis shift that the Great Commission demands, I want to draw attention to one of my favorite missionaries in church history. His work shows, I think, what can happen when a life is ordered by the call to preach the gospel. His emphasis on reaching the world's *un-heards* was revolutionary during his time and would be in ours as well. I hope that as we look at these proposed emphasis shifts, the example of this missionary will be both instructive and challenging for us.

William Carey is often called the Father of Modern Missions because of the dramatic ways his ministry influenced the church's worldwide disciple-making strategy and method. His missionary work ignited a flurry of movement from places with a high 'reached' factor to relatively unreached places. But this man, though he certainly helped instigate a major shift in the church's attitude towards the Great Commission in the two ensuing centuries, is not the one I wish to highlight.[22]

For the same reasons that earned the moniker for Carey, I think Philip the Evangelist might be aptly called the Father of Primitive Missions! Due in large part to the work of which we're given a glimpse in Acts 8, the early church breaks through significant barriers to cross-cultural gospel ministry, barriers that continue to be broken throughout the rest of the book. Philip's is the first account we're given in Acts of someone bringing the gospel to half-Jewish Samaritans and then to straight-up Gentiles. The size of the geographic, cultural and racial obstacles that Philip overcame to do so is difficult for us in the twenty-first century to grasp. Modern people may take for granted that people of other races and cultures have equal dignity and value; there was no such conviction in Philip's day. In the face of such challenges, he helped open a door that has remained open for the past two thousand years. In fact, it's the door that we walked through when we, if we are Gentiles, came to Christ!

At the beginning of Acts 8, the chapter that features Philip prominently, it seems that the early church is not yet fully appreciating the implications of Christ's last command. Subsequent to the martyrdom of Stephen, many disciples scatter outwards from Jerusalem, preaching the gospel boldly, but with a restriction (see Acts 8:1). Luke tells us later on that this dissemination of believers only preached to Jewish people (see 11:19). Apparently, it was an assumption of the early church to a great extent at this time that the work of disciple making was supposed to be limited to ethnic Israel. But Philip's brain seems to work differently. Maybe it was because he was steeped in the Old Testament and knew that the age of blessing to all ages had arrived in Christ (see 8:35). Maybe he remembered some of Jesus' fascinating interactions with Samaritans (see Luke 17:11-19; John 4). Or maybe he had reflected on Christ's words in the Great Commission more fully than others. Maybe he just missed the Evangelism Methodology class in seminary and didn't know any better. Either way, he intentionally goes to find some Samaritans (see Acts 8:5)! It would be interesting to know what other believers at the time would have said if he had asked beforehand what they thought about it. They likely would have thought it a vain enterprise, a secondarily important venture or even a theologically aberrant undertaking. But, amazingly, a great number of Samaritans respond in faith to the Gospel of Christ (see 8:6-8)!

When the apostles hear of the shocking response to Philip's preaching, Peter and John are sent over to Samaria to see what has happened with their own eyes (see 8:14). Far from rebuking Philip for his indiscriminate disciple making, they pray for the Samaritans to receive the Spirit and continue the teaching work that Philip started (see 8:15-17, 25a). After bestowing these blessings, Peter and John check out and head for home; but it would appear that their own perspective has shifted. For Luke tells us that they themselves made a tour of Samaritan villages on the way to Jerusalem, preaching the gospel to all who would listen (see Acts 8:25b)! Clearly the episode into which Philip had brought them forced them to reconsider a thing or two. This is the first of several accounts in Acts where Peter and the apostles are made increasingly aware of the implications of the great age that has dawned in Christ's glorification (see 10:44-48; 15:5-21). But you might say Philip is ahead of the curve.

Philip wasn't retiring out of the race to the *unheards* yet, either! Is it any wonder that when the Holy Spirit wants someone to talk to an Ethiopian, he passes over many more illustrious disciples in favor of the ambitious evangelist (see 8:26)? It's unclear where Philip was when the call to go to the desert came, but it's likely he was still occupied with his disciple-making labors in Samaria. If so, any believer in Jerusalem was much closer to the eunuch than Philip was, there in the Samaritan territory to the north (for that matter, the eunuch had set out *from* Jerusalem!). Either way, there doesn't seem to be anything to distinguish Philip as a particularly qualified candidate to talk to an Ethiopian politician, except, of course, for Philip's now-established record of groundbreaking disciple-making endeavors! So he is the one recruited.

To see just how unusual Philip was, let's do a quick comparison of Philip's approach to the eunuch here in Acts 8 with Peter's approach to the Roman centurion Cornelius two chapters later. Both Cornelius and the eunuch relate to Israel in the same way: they're both "God-fearers," that is, Gentiles who worship the one true God of the Jewish people, the God of the Old Testament Scriptures, yet who remain formally outside of the Jewish community (due to noncompliance with stipulations like dietary laws and circumcision). The eunuch comes to Jerusalem to worship the God of the Jews (see Acts 8:27-28). Cornelius' household fears and prays to the same God (see 10:1-2). Yet when the Spirit commands Peter to go along with Cornelius' messengers, he seems completely at a loss to know what to do in this situation. He even asks Cornelius' family what they sent for him for (see 10:29)! It is only after Cornelius relays the content of the vision he saw that it finally seems to dawn on Peter that the message of the gospel may be of some use to these Gentiles (see 10:30-33)! His speech seems to be less a sermon than his own reasoning-out of what he sees unfolding before him (see 10:34-43). No matter—the message of forgiveness through the gospel is communicated, and Cornelius and his family believe (see 10:44-48)!

Philip, on the other hand, isn't called "the Evangelist" for nothing (see 21:8)! Philip seems to have been given less information about what his mission to the eunuch entailed than Peter was given in his rooftop vision. He also seems to have had less reason to believe that the gospel should have anything to do with this eunuch than Peter would have had about Cornelius (who, from the information we're given, seems to have been a bit more "into" Judaism than the eunuch). But Philip hightails it over to the chariot and immediately engages the eunuch concerning the content of the Scripture he was reading (see 8:29-35). He wastes no time getting to the heart of the matter: Jesus! No additional prodding is needed to convince Philip that the eunuch is a viable disciple-making target. He knows what to do, and this is certainly why he was the one dispatched on this history-making mission.

Where does the chapter leave Philip? Not surprisingly, exported (by the Spirit's means) to—you guessed it—another cluster of *unheards* (see 8:39-40). Philip finds himself at Azotus, where he once again preaches to everyone he can find, winding his way from town to town until he comes to Caesarea, one of the larger cities in the Roman Empire at the time, where he seems to take up an extended residence (see Acts 21:8). Little wonder—a city of tens of thousands of *unheards* seems like exactly the kind of place where a guy like Philip would want to settle down!

Philip paves the way for future outreach to *unheards* all over the world. His priorities are clearly different from those of most of his contemporaries, and that is what makes him so anxious to reach Samaritans, Ethiopians and Caesareans. This in particular is why I want us to see the example of Philip. Like William Carey centuries later, Philip was not simply following along with the typical policies and procedures of his day. He was ordering his life by the Commission with dramatic results.

As we're talking about our local churches today adjusting some of their priorities, you may find yourself in a situation like one of these two great missionaries of the past. What do you do if your church doesn't place a great emphasis on the unreached people of the world? Well, if we follow Philip's example, the answer would seem to be changing your own personal priorities to target the *unheards*. Much good will come of this, both for those unbelievers to whom you personally give the gospel, and for those believers who see the fruits of your unusual emphases and take steps of their own toward the world.

So let's take a closer look at some of the emphases that the Great Commission calls us to adjust, and may the Lord of the harvest send forth laborers with the heart of Philip into the ripest, most overgrown patches of the worldwide field!

8

Off the Cultural Mandate, Onto Disciple Making

Are there many endeavors whereby believers equally bring glory to God?

The cultural mandate refers to the earliest commission given to mankind. It is a command even older than the Fall! As we still live in a world imprisoned by sin, any biblical information available to us about the way the world and mankind worked in those first days before the corruption of sin is sure to awaken our curiosity. After all, there are only a couple chapters of such information in Scripture; the cultural mandate is a key feature of those chapters. It was man's orientation to the wonderful world he had been planted in. Within this orientation, God outlined for Adam what his existence was about and the work that he had been assigned to do. If the Fall had not occurred, mankind as a whole would still be joyfully living out these words.

The Original Blueprint

So what exactly is entailed by this orientation, often referred to as "the cultural mandate"? When God created Adam and Eve after His own image and placed them in the garden of Eden,

135

He gave them some responsibilities: to cultivate the earth, to rule the earth and to fill the earth by multiplying their offspring (see Gen. 1:28). Some, following the biblical prophet Hosea, have even referred to this as God's covenant with Adam, the stipulations that bound them together in relationship to one another. Adam was to till and cultivate and rule the creation of God. God would be all for him, providing even his daily food in the trees that grew all over the garden. Speaking of trees, their relationship included a prohibition (as all genuine relationships must): Adam was not to eat of the Tree of the Knowledge of Good and Evil. If this condition was broken, there would be dire consequences.

Let's go back over this content quickly and attempt to distill it down to some basic elements. Doing so will allow us to see God's intentions in creation and what that in turn means for us, hundreds of generations after Adam.

First, the cultural mandate is about dominion. God commands man to work, making himself more and more the creation's master, the earth more and more his servant. This authority is to be first utilized in the garden of Eden, where Adam is to act as a caretaker. Doubtless, with the growth of Adam's family this task of subduing the world would find expansion into every realm of the creation. This cultural mandate, then, shows that work predates mankind's collapse into sin and is therefore a basically good thing. Work has God-glorifying value, for when we as people labor in the world God has created, we reenact God's work of bringing order out of chaos.

Second, the cultural mandate is about multiplication. God commands man to fill up the world with people. Man has deep intrinsic worth as he is the masterpiece of God's creation, painted in vibrant hues of divine likeness. The Creator, God, plans to display His glory through the panorama of human diversity, with each individual person acting like a uniquely-cut diamond, refracting and reflecting the infinitely radiant beauty of His attributes. The larger Adam's family grows, the greater God's glory is shown! So the cultural mandate here tells us something about the true value of a human life in God's eyes. Life is to be regarded as precious in our eyes, and we are to seek to guard, cherish, honor, respect, enrich and encourage its propagation. The cultural mandate leaves no room for misanthropy.

Third, the cultural mandate is about relationship. God isn't interested in filling the earth with human beings indifferent to His existence. Rather, He wants His worshipers multiplied—people who have submitted themselves joyfully to His rule, trusting His word and believing Him to be their supreme good. Adam is given a command to follow, which serves as a means whereby he continually expresses his trust in God to be God. All the bounty of the garden is given to Adam and Eve to thankfully enjoy as they commune with God daily. So the cultural mandate reveals that man's primary identity is that of a worshiper of God. Anything less than grateful trust in our Creator is rebellion against His original design.

It seems, then, that the cultural mandate provides us with information about God's original plan for mankind: that they would rule over His creation, filling it with His true worshipers. This charter makes clear for us what we mean by Adam being the pinnacle of God's creation, the very centerpiece of His plan to glorify Himself in the universe. It is also instructive for us as we begin to grasp the climax to which God intends to bring the drama of human history. God isn't accustomed to failure. He hasn't once managed to lose! So if He plans to make a humanity like the one described in the cultural mandate, it wouldn't be wise to bet against Him!

The Great Competitor

I find that it is not uncommon nowadays to encounter young people in gospel-preaching churches who have a working understanding of this divine plan for humanity. In accordance with this oldest of mandates, they have resolved to glorify God through their life's work, whatever it may be. They understand that their lives cannot be divided into the holy and the profane. All is to be directed into making much of God. Whereas many Christians historically have mostly thought of their service to God as limited to their ministry roles in the church, this youngest generation of believers in the West has been challenged to consider how their decorating, their masonry, their entrepreneurship, their investing, their cooking or their coaching fulfill God's directive to be the masters of creation.

While I heartily rejoice over these positive results that have come from making much of God's original plan for mankind, I believe that there has also been an unfortunate side effect. Specifically, this emphasis has caused some to perceive worldwide disciple making as one potential variant of the obedient Christian life, rather than as an underlying framework that describes all of our work in the world. This perception manifests itself in an unexamined assumption that they do not need to be exported to bring God maximum glory from their lives (by way of reminder, by *exported* I mean 'to change their geographic location to put themselves in a better position to make disciples'). In other words, these young believers feel secure in their decision to stay right where they are and not give much serious consideration to moving toward the *unheards* in another part of the world. Their awareness of the cultural mandate seems to remove the urgency and priority of the Great Commission. Why would this be so?

Well, in some ways, the cultural mandate just seems "bigger" than the Great Commission. It holds the position of seniority over all other directives of God to mankind and speaks in sweeping terms about the purpose of humanity, more broadly even than the Great Commission. So if we're picking a paradigm or deciding on a charter for our existence as God's people, the cultural mandate seems to be a better fit. The work of the Great Commission, then, would be a subset of the work of the cultural mandate. You could express this perspective like this: all work glorifies God and worldwide disciple making is one kind of work that glorifies God. This would mean, of course, that believers who are not busy about making disciples will nevertheless prove to be obedient followers of Christ.

I, along with many others who often find themselves speaking as advocates for the world's unreached, have found that a strong emphasis on the cultural mandate can act as impervious armor against the pricks of the Great Commission. When the need for worldwide disciple making is pressed hard upon this younger generation, they often seem baffled by the insistence that missions could have any special claim upon their lives. If I explain to a brother or sister that I think becoming an exported disciple maker would be more honoring to God than remaining in their current post, a blank look is very often my only reward. "But I thought," they begin, "that all work is equally glorious in God's eyes. Aren't there an infinite number of ways to glorify God, and isn't making disciples simply one of those ways?" Truly, many of them believe that it is no more God-honoring to proclaim the gospel to someone you work with than it is to show up to work on time and work hard the whole time you're on the clock. They are persuaded that some people have the gift of evangelism, while others have the gift of architecture or the gift of banking or the gift of mother-hood.

The battle cry of world evangelization falls upon deaf ears because they see whatever they are currently doing (or aspiring to do in the future) as equally worthy of their efforts and abilities. They believe that a believer only needs to discover how his work is a fulfillment of the cultural mandate, and he is to then feel fulfilled in the glory brought to God by every swing of his hammer or stroke on his keyboard; nothing greater need be considered.

While some of the more ardent and thoughtful proponents of the cultural mandate will say this is a misrepresentation of their position (I have no doubt it is), it is unfortunately the message that is many times received by the younger generation in our churches. In other words, the cultural mandate is perceived to be an alternative to the Great Commission. To put it more accurately, perhaps, the Great Commission is seen as a subheading underneath the cultural mandate. Some people make disciples, some proclaim the gospel, but others are lawyers, accountants, land developers and software engineers.

I sense this competition whenever I talk to students about the need for gospel proclamation around the world. It's not uncommon for one of them to say something like, "But can't God be glorified through my chosen occupation? It's not just missionaries who are being faithful to Christ's commands!" Of course, they are very right, but I want you to notice that the one truth can be used to defuse the tension of the other. When believers (of any age) feel particularly burdened by the command of Christ to carry the gospel to the world, they can look to this other truth to offer them an alternative plan for glorifying God with their lives. Therefore, I say that the divine mandate given in Genesis and the divine mandate given in the Gospels seem to be in competition with one another for emphasis in our churches.

The solution to this problem is not to deny the true and vital relevance of the cultural mandate. Instead, since the Commission and the mandate seem to be in juxtaposition to one another, both offering a paradigm to view our whole work on this earth, we must reexamine our potentially faulty understanding of their relationship to one another. We should not think that two such paradigmatic charters from the same Lord, though given so many years apart from each other, should stand completely independent of each other. Where shall we begin in this quest to understand the relationship between these two charters?

The Hiccup in the Plan

Granted that the cultural mandate certainly is the original charter for mankind, it would be worth our time to consider just how that has worked out so far. The cultural mandate may very well show us the end to which humans were meant to direct themselves, but how exactly can they hope to arrive there? Our experience as members of the human race tells us undoubtedly that something has gone seriously awry since the cultural mandate was given to our first parents. Until we discover what that something is, it will be impossible for us to understand the relationship between God's original cultural mandate and His Great Commission thousands of years later.

The problem is that, a mere three chapters into the Bible, a giant wrench was stuck into the gears of humanity's engine. Adam and Eve were created to be like a mighty locomotive, charging down the track laid before them by God in the cultural mandate. But when they sinned against God's command, the train of man's divine mission derailed. The Fall was not just a little speed bump in the road that shook mankind momentarily before we continued on our merry way down the track. It was, rather, a catastrophic destruction of our capacity to glorify God in the way He planned! Man is not like a reliable vehicle due for an oil change and regular maintenance; he is like a crumpled car still tumbling end-over-end after a high-speed collision. We must not minimize this fact as we contemplate the mandate's relevance for today. We must not look the other way when we pass the wreckage. When we look at Adam and Eve after the Fall, we are not supposed to think, "Oh, that was an unfortunate blunder—now back to glorifying God!" We are supposed to cry out in horror, "How can anyone have survived that to glorify God again?"

Do you see the wreckage from Adam and Eve's fall? First, they were made to have dominion over the creation, but now the ground man tills will stubbornly resist his rule (see Gen. 2:15; 3:17-19). When we think about the vast strides that science and technology have made in the process of earth-domination over the ensuing millennia, let us also reflect on the natural disasters, the uncured diseases, the uninhabitable environments and the huge gaps in our knowledge that are so characteristic of man's experience on the earth. Second, they were made to fill the earth with living reflections of God's image, but now childbirth is a terribly painful ordeal, and death rules absolutely over mankind (see 1:28; 3:16). Seven billion inhabitants may seem like a lot to us—but imagine if Adam and every man and woman that had lived since him were still alive, never killing each other in wars, never aborting their children, never succumbing to sickness, never weeping in infertility and never slowing down in old age! And third, they were made to walk in perfect fellowship with God, but now that they are banished from His garden, approach to God requires bloody sacrifice and their offspring are born with the same twisted nature that now resides in their hearts (see Gen. 3:21-24; 4:4). Their first attempts at raising children to be worshipers of God are typical of all history since: their first son kills their second (see 4:8-12), over what else, but his own unwillingness to worship God!

In the rest of the Old Testament, we see repeated attempts to steer devastated humanity down the road of the cultural mandate. Adam and Eve keep tilling, keep having babies and keep trying to walk with God. But within a few centuries, their children have become so evil that God resolves to destroy them all with a flood of judgment (see 6:5-7). The cultural mandate fails.

Noah comes off the ark with his family and with a fresh start at the work of subduing, multiplying and worshiping. But Noah's offspring set their own agenda and are soon hard at work building a tower in rebellion against God's directives. God wants them out subduing and multiplying; they want to stay in and build up to heaven (see 11:1-8). Again, the cultural mandate fails.

The family of Abraham is chosen out of all the families of the earth to be multiplied greatly and become a blessing to all peoples (see 12:1-3). But between Abraham and Isaac's lies bringing infertility upon a pagan people (see 20; 26:6-11) and Simeon and Levi's slaying the Shechemites in deceit (see 34:18-31), the first few generations are more of a curse to the surrounding nations than a blessing. Failure again and again.

Israel's miraculous escape from slavery, their miraculous sustenance in the wilderness, their miraculous conquest of Canaan and their miraculous survival despite multiplied oppressors in the period of the judges reveal that they, too, were attempting to move in the direction of the cultural mandate to increase the worshipers of God and their rule over the earth. But they repeatedly disregard the worship prescribed by the Lord, and the result is oppression, war, plagues and death. The cultural mandate stalls out again (see Deut. 4:1-40; 7:1-26; 28:1-68; 30:11-20).

Israel rises to new heights with the establishment of a monarchy. Under David and his son Solomon, real progress seems to be made in fulfilling the cultural mandate. The worship of God is carefully guarded, the people prosper and the earth yields its riches to them (see 2 Sam. 7:1-29; 1 Kings 8:1-9:9; 10:1-29). But it lasts no longer than Solomon's youth. From the time he is old until the people are taken into captivity a few hundred years later, the kingdom tumbles wildly off course, lost in idolatry and violence, returning to the tracks only briefly every couple of generations or so (see 1 Kings 11:1-13, 2 Kings 17:7-23) . The cultural mandate never seems more hopeless than when the worshipers of God sit finally in exile from the Promised Land.

Over and over again, man has steered back onto the road only to spin out of control and off the opposite side of the road. So it's safe to say that the cultural mandate is like an engine that has been rebuilt time and time again, but always with the same result: breakdown. Man redoubles his efforts to subdue the earth, multiply his seed and even to worship God; but the Fall wins out every time.

It is absurd to simply maintain that the cultural mandate is the purpose of our existence without reckoning with how the Fall has affected our ability to perform it! It's like a football coach hearing that his star player has been paralyzed and burnt in a terrible accident and then proceeding to include him on the starting roster for Friday's big game. He can wheel the poor kid out onto the field if he wants, but he shouldn't expect any points to be scored. Any expectations for humanity will fall similarly flat. The Fall has made us thoroughly incapable of glorifying God in our work. It has undone our ability to honor and value the dignity of human life. It has also absolutely ruined us for worship. The engine is fried. This means that we can't draw a straight line from the cultural mandate to ourselves. When the line passes through Genesis 3, it becomes tangled and faded. Because of this "hiccup" in the plan, our application of the cultural mandate to our own lives must be more nuanced.

The Redemption of the Mandate

Of course, as we said at the beginning, the disrepair of the engine is in no wise a threat to the fulfillment of God's plan for mankind. Humanity totaling itself was not a surprise to God. If the engine is burnt out, God must certainly have a plan for its eventual, ultimate rebuild—the one that will restore the children of Adam and Eve to their divinely mandated course.

That plan is nothing other than the gospel. Christ came and showed what a whole, unbroken engine looks like. Zealously committed without reserve to the glory of His Father, Jesus lived a life of unswerving worship, yet died in the fiery crash that should have claimed our lives. By trusting in this work of Christ's, wrecked men are reborn, recreated, reforged, rebuilt. With new life within, they are finally able to start glorifying God in the way that He originally intended—with their work, with their relationships and with their worship.

Here's where the Commission comes in. Having traced the cultural mandate's line thus far, hopefully we are in a better position to see the relationship it bears to this apparently new command of God. The redeeming Lord, risen from the grave, commands His church to take this good news into all the world, making more disciples who will be capable of glorifying God in their work, their relationships and their worship. No matter their racial or economic background, the gospel is to be delivered to them so they might be recovered from the twisted hull of their ruined souls. This, as we have already seen, must be taken as the basis of all the church's ministry to the world.

Now the connection between commission and mandate becomes clearer. We could illustrate it like this: the cultural mandate given in Genesis is like the original road that man was to follow before he got off course; the Great Commission is the new, "recalculated" course that the GPS has drawn to take us to our original destination, out of the mess into which we have got ourselves. In more practical terms, the Great Commission is a specific, updated set of instructions given to the church about what they are to do in this point in history to achieve the ends for which God created mankind, outlined even before the Fall. The scope of the cultural mandate arches from the first day of man's creation to his eternal state with God. The Great Commission, however, tells us what we as God's redeemed, regenerated people are to do at this particular point in that arch. During this age between the first and second comings of Christ, the cultural mandate can only be obeyed in the context of the Great Commission.

This is not to say that the believer's work at this point in history bears no similarity to the work originally prescribed in the cultural mandate. We are still concerned with dominion, multiplication, and relation to God. But remember how the sweeping terms of the cultural mandate, "subdue the earth" and "have dominion over it" (see Gen. 1:28), are made more specific for Adam's immediate time in Genesis 2:15-20? God puts Adam in charge of taking care of the garden of Eden. He sets him the task of naming all the animals. He tells him which trees are for eating, and which tree is restricted. These are specific instructions that tell Adam exactly how he is to be busy about the work of the cultural mandate at this time. Now the church, the body of Christ, has also been given a specific way to work for mankind's dominion, multiplication and worship in our own time. Let's think for a second how the work of the Great Commission relates to the goals of the cultural mandate.

First of all, consider how the disciple-making mission causes men to worship and glorify God. In Second Corinthians 4:15, Paul says that God's grace spreading to more and more people leads those who believe to give thanks to God, which in turn magnifies God's worth. In other words, the more people who receive salvation, the more glorious God appears. In Romans, Paul tells us that Christ welcomed us into his family to bring praise and glory to God (see Rom. 15:7). The mercy people receive in the gospel, then, causes them to worship God. When Paul and Barnabas narrowly avoided becoming the objects of false worship themselves, they cried out to stop the people, declaring that they had come to turn them from worship of vanities to worship of a living God (see Acts 14:15). So it is by the preaching of the gospel whereby idolaters come to relate rightly to God. One more example is in John 4:23, when Jesus tells the Samaritan woman that the time for doing away with geographical distinctions has come, and that the true worshipers will worship God in the person of Jesus Christ. Thus, under the New Covenant which Christ has established, true worship is possible. People can reconnect to God in a way that should have been impossible after the catastrophe in Eden. Therefore, when we obey the Great Commission, we are obeying the cultural mandate in our time, for we are increasing God's worldwide worship.

Second, consider how the disciple-making mission is an act of multiplication, of filling the world with those true worshipers. Paul is accustomed in his letters to speak of the believers in the churches he has planted as his spiritual children (see 1 Cor. 4:15; 2 Cor. 12:14; 1 Thess. 2:7). Take, for instance, Galatians 4:19. Paul says that he is in the agony of childbirth, suffering hardship and never resting until he is assured that Christ is within them. The apostle John shares Paul's view. In his epistles he also speaks of his audience as if they were his offspring (see 1 John 2:1; 3 John 1:4). Of course, Jesus was the one who initiated this kind of terminology, referring in John 3 to a new birth that grown men must also experience and referring to his followers as his "little children" (John 13:33). What all this shows is that today, the multiplication that we are most concerned with comes not by physical birth, but by spiritual birth. As we obey the Great Commission, we are truly obeying the cultural mandate for our time, because we are working to fill the earth up with people who know and glorify the Lord.

Thirdly, consider how the disciple-making mission is labor—a task of reaping and sowing upon which all of creation hangs. That's quite a mouthful, so let's take it a bite at a time. To start, missions is a task. Paul says the gospel ministry is about striving with all of our energies to lead someone to maturity in Christ (see Col. 1:28-29). The task of worldwide disciple making is a difficult one which demands that we toil with all our might. One of the most consistent metaphors used in Scripture to describe this toil is that of a farmer sowing seed and reaping a harvest. In First Corinthians, Paul compares disciple makers to farmers planting and watering, working tirelessly as they hope for a good harvest (see 1 Cor. 3:5-8). Though thousands of years removed from our first father, Adam, we as sons of God have not yet finished our work of cultivation—in this time, our seed is the word of God and the field is the world's *unheards*.

Just as Adam's work in the garden was but the beginning of his worldwide dominion, so too the drama of God's redemption of a people from out of the world is an inaugural fulfillment of the future redemption of all creation. Romans 8 leads us to believe that those who have been born again are but the "firstfruits" of God's redeeming work (see Rom. 8:18-23). When our glory eventually is revealed (in victorious resurrection life), then all of creation will be simultaneously released from its own bondage to realize the glory envisioned in the cultural mandate. Now, if Paul was interested in the redemption of creation in this age, this would be the perfect place to mention it! But he reiterates that in this time the Spirit's redeeming work takes place in the hearts of men. Creation will have to wait anxiously for its turn. So we find that the Great Commission is deeply concerned with mankind's dominion over the earth, yet it insists that in this present time, the work that we are to engage in to effect that dominion is the hard work of sowing and reaping for the sake of the sons of God. Missions is about redeeming the sons of God, without whom creation will not be redeemed.

I conclude, then, that it is improper to force missions into a subheading beneath the cultural mandate. The key aspects of the cultural mandate are all preserved in the Great Commission. The work of worldwide disciple making is not just a part of the cultural mandate. Rather, the Great Commission is the application of the cultural mandate to our post-cross, pre-return-of-Christ age! It is the work whereby we the church glorify God and multiply His worshipers. Missions, then, is not one of the

God-glorifying works approved by the cultural mandate. It is the only work that will make the world idealized in the cultural mandate anything more than a joke or a dream. As John Piper famously wrote, "Missions exists because worship doesn't."[23] The point of the Great Commission is to bring the cultural mandate back into the realm of possibility by restoring mankind back to the road of worship that we lost so long ago. Whether in Papua New Guinea, Libya or Ecuador, our efforts of disciple making among the *unheards* is, in this age, our pressing toward the original end of humanity's existence.

All for God's Greatest Glory

I hope it's clear by now that I do not want to be an opponent of the Creator's original plan for humanity; as God is my help, I want desperately to work toward that exact end here in China. That end, however, will only be reached by following the re-charted course laid for us by the Great Commission GPS. I don't love disciple-making missions instead of the cultural mandate; I love disciple-making missions because I love the cultural mandate! If we long for the world to be redeemed in the way described in God's original plan, we must strive tirelessly along the road that he has mapped out to lead back to that plan. In other words, we must change our emphasis. We must use more teaching time to talk about the Great Commission. We must spend more money on the work of worldwide disciple making. We must invest more manpower into missions. We must also put more planning into reaching the *unheards* than we do into the cultural mandate. At the very least, we need to teach the cultural mandate in the context of the Great Commission.

As with so many other good things, we as believers must learn to obey God in our occupations without reducing the whole of our mission down to them. We ought to do these things and not leave the others undone! My point is not that Christians should be indifferent about their occupations, but rather that they should do them faithfully, as unto the Lord, not unto men, and at the same time strive fervently with every resource at their disposal (including their occupations!) for the mission of global disciple making.

You might recall at this juncture that Paul told the Corinthians to do all for the glory of God, right down to what they ate and drank (see 1 Cor. 10:31). Doesn't this mean that there is a way for Christians to glorify God in every aspect of our lives? Definitely. But surely it would be bizarre to think of Paul as telling the Corinthian church that their main goal in life is to bring glory to God by eating and drinking! The thrust of his argument is designed to make them say, "Come on, Paul, surely you're exaggerating! Do you think that sticking food in my stomach really registers on the scale of God's glory?" In other words, Paul assumes that they think of eating and drinking as small things, not main things!

Then, in the same paragraph, he explains how it is that choices about food and drink register on God's glory scale (see 10:31-33)! Paul says that in this small matter of eating meats offered to idols, they should act as he does. He personally foregoes certain freedoms so that his ministry to others would be amplified. He seeks to please all men, prioritizing their benefit over his own. What benefit is he attempting to bring to people by his abstaining from these freedoms? Salvation! This means that Paul orders even the seemingly insignificant details of his life (such as what kinds of food he will eat) in such a way as to cause people to be more receptive to the gospel. So Paul is saying in these verses, "Even little choices such as these are an opportunity to give up our rights and make disciples for the glory of God!" Again we find that it is in people being saved that God is most glorified!

It is this sacrificing of his own good for theirs that makes his eating and drinking so glorious to God. Paul doesn't attempt to show them that the action of eating food is a God-glorifying thing because eating dead animals is part of exercising our dominion over the earth as per the cultural mandate. Rather, he connects his choices in this matter to disciple making as per the Great Commission! I certainly don't mean that there are no other ways that the little things in our lives bring glory to God. I do mean that glory comes in degrees, and that the greatest God-glorifying work in our time entails bearing witness to the gospel before unbelievers. I fear that the present generation is learning to do all for the glory of God—all, that is, except for the greatest task whereby we are to glorify God in this time: in bearing witness to the gospel in all the world! This is the glory that Paul was encouraging the Corinthians to pursue, and it is the glory for which the Western church today desperately needs a vision.

The youngest generation in our churches needs to be taught how they can best glorify God with their lives. Jesus' last words to His followers before His ascension were not something like, "Guys, I want you to glorify me on the earth. So get creative! Dream up a bunch of ways to make this happen!" On the contrary, He laid out the particular actions of the Great Commission as our role to play in redeeming man's God-glorifying potential.

When young believers are taught that writing a blog with theological perspective, or establishing a business that operates ethically, or seeking the election of a conservative political candidate or sharing the gospel with *unheards* in Bangladesh are all equally powerful ways to bring glory to God, is it any wonder that only a tiny number volunteer to go to Bangladesh? If I can do just as much good here (with more amenities) what motivation is there for me to go there? But when young men and women are advised to seek God's maximum glory from their lives' work, then we will begin to see movement toward the darkest places on earth.

Furthermore, believers must be taught that no one can opt out of the work of disciple making. Just as the cultural mandate is universal in its scope, so too the Great Commission delineates the way in which all of God's people are to be busy glorifying Him. Glorifying God by the diligent manner in which you work is commendable, but incomplete. Building a charitable business brings glory to God, but it's not the ultimate work he has for you to do. Thinking of yourself as glorifying God primarily by disciple making and secondarily by being a businessman means that you will make some decisions that will hurt your business and be incomprehensible to your colleagues. Conversely, if you think of your glorification efforts as primarily taking place in the realm of your business operations, you will at many points resign yourself to ineffectiveness at making disciples. No matter how noble the work—be it motherhood or management—it does not preclude you from the work of making disciples out of unbelievers.

Cultural renewal, environmental conservation, educational progress, political reform, economic growth and good parenting are all things that we as believers may rejoice in as fragmentary glimpses of the world as it should and will be when God has His rightful place. Nonetheless, we must never confuse such things with our mission in this era: making disciples out of *unheards*. Sadly, many Western Christians are passionate advocates of some of the abovementioned issues in their home country, but couldn't tell you the first thing about the state of the church in North Africa. Many churches plead with God far more fervently concerning upcoming votes and their children's education than they do about the millions who have never heard the gospel. It is so much easier for congregations to celebrate the small-scale redemption that they see in local cultural renewal than it is for them to get excited about the cosmic-scale redemption that can be seen in the discipleship of *unheards* around the world. It's time to turn this emphasis on its head. God's glory demands it.

9

Off Calling, Onto Volunteering

Are some Christians specially called to serve as missionaries?

Though it would have made a mess of the book's structure, I almost think that this chapter should have come first. How we as Christians are to perceive and obey God's will for us is one of the issues most integrally related to the church's exporting capacity. To put it another way, an obedient Christian won't decide to move until they believe that's what God wants them to do or, as we often say, that it is His will that they go. Few believers are going to wake up today and decide over their morning coffee that it would be fun or fulfilling to sell their house, say goodbye to their families and move to the other side of the world. Such a decision would fly in the face of all our instincts. So if we're going to go, it's got to be because we believe that God wants us to go.

That's why I say this chapter perhaps ought to be out front. As long as a believer believes God wants him to stay, no quantity of reasons to go will dislodge him. All the arguments of the previous chapters fall on deaf ears. Thus, the problem I want to battle in this chapter is simply this: most Christians do not believe that God wants them to go to another place as missionaries—and most isn't 51 percent. We're clearly talking about the overwhelming majority of Western Christians here. To use the "will of God" language that we will examine in this chapter, they do not believe that God is calling them into missions.

Please don't read me as saying that most Christians do not care about missions. In fact, I find the opposite to be true! When I am a guest at churches in the United States, I am struck by the number of members I encounter who wholeheartedly believe in the value of missionary endeavors.

Deciding Between Good and God's Best

What is so striking about these genuine lovers of missions is how few of them believe that they personally belong on the mission field! It is becoming more common, I find, when talking to a young believer, to discover a true passion for the world's unreached. They're aware of the persecuted church. They're educated about unengaged people groups. They're conscious of the progress of the gospel in various countries. Detecting this passion, I almost always stick my foot in my mouth and ask, "So are you interested in becoming a missionary?"

"No, I don't think I'm called."

So I'm learning that the nature of this mysterious call, the elusive will of God for our lives, is one of the key issues that must be addressed if we are to break down the dam between the reservoir of Western Christianity and the gospel-parched, Word-bereft lands that lie past our horizons. If I were a much more talented writer and could somehow marshal every argument, every reason, every motivation for your exportation to the world's *unheards*, then march them like an army against the walls of your will, your view of God's call alone would enable you to repel wave after wave of pleas. God's calling works like an all-powerful trump card, canceling out all other factors that might be considered in your decision.

The places where our perspective on the will of God for our lives is most influential are those points of decision about which the Bible does not speak conclusively. We stand at a fork in the road, and neither path seems to be explicitly right or wrong. Marry what's-her-name or don't marry her. Pursue postgraduate education or get a job. Become a doctor or become something else. Get the face tattoo or make a good impression on everyone. We are struggling to determine what it is that God wants us to do—which of multiple apparently good paths He wants us to take.

The crossroads that perplex us are never a choice between good and evil. In such matters, a Christian doesn't need to pray for direction; he needs to pray for strength to do what is right. That's why we need not linger at the intersection of involvement in missions and detachment from missions. The Great Commission barricades the latter path and points neon arrows down the former! Once we've committed ourselves to walk the road of obedience to the Great Commission, however, we soon discover that there are a hundred more forks waiting ahead, none of which are as clearly demarcated. These decisions are about the specific nature of our personal role in worldwide missions, and are not directly settled by God's instruction to us in Scripture. At these intersections, we must pause. We are not now considering whether or not God wants us to preach the gospel to unbelievers, but which unbelievers we should set ourselves to reach.

How do I know if God wants me to be an exported missionary or not? The answer commonly endorsed by modern believers is, "If he wants you to go, he will call you to go." What they mean by call, of course, is that God will speak to these believers through unique circumstances, through impressions, through dreams, through opportunities or some other special means, and inform them of His intentions for their lives. This emphasis on the call is not just at the popular level, either. This past week I heard a staff member of a very large American mission board insist that the most important qualification for missionary candidates is that they give a good testimony of their call.

Though most believers may agree that the unreached condition of hundreds of millions around the world is outrageous and unacceptable, they will assume that God wants them to remain where they are unless they receive some sort of divine confirmation that they are one of the special few who should go. Allow me, then, to assert a corollary to the problem I mentioned above: unless many believers' view of God's calling drastically changes, they will not go as exported missionaries.

It seems that there are really only a couple possibilities to explain so many nearly-empty harvest fields in the world:

1. God is only calling a few Christians to go as missionaries, because he doesn't want everyone in our generation to hear the gospel.

2. God is calling a sufficient number of workers, but many, if not almost all, of them are being disobedient to that call.

3. We have seriously misunderstood what it means to be called by God.

Out of those three possibilities, I find the third to be by far the most compelling. It is for this reason that I hope, in these next pages, to suggest some ways that our emphasis on God's call might be in error. You may not agree with some of the details of my analysis, but I hope you will agree with the verdict. I know there are several aspects of this issue, and relevant Scriptures that will not be given their due treatment below, but I must try to stick to the path before us: the calling of God as it relates most directly to the Great Commission's demands on our lives.

Four Approaches to Finding God's Call

Before jumping into a bunch of arguments for adjusting our view of God's will, it might be helpful to ask what exactly it means when people say that they are called or not called to do something. Inconveniently, there is a wide range of answers to that question. People may mean very different things indeed. It is astonishing how many teachers and preachers who otherwise consistently exhibit deliberate care in their theological statements seem to throw caution to the wind when talking about God's call. It's often quite difficult to know what on earth someone means when they say, "God called me to go to China," or "God told me to marry my wife."

The situation in the pew is even more desperate. Even though anyone who grew up in church has heard dozens of sermons on the subject, most believers still find it hard to articulate their own opinion on the matter clearly. So most believers aren't really flying the flag of any one school of thought. Their own muddled, customized version of God's will has mostly been cobbled together from bits and pieces of teaching they've heard over the years.

Usually when a Christian talks about being called to do something, he is implying that, in the absence of a scriptural road map telling him what to do, some other method has been used to determine which is the right path to take. The Bible doesn't say whether a missionary should minister in northeast China or in southwest China, so we relegate such questions to the realm of calling. How do believers go about determining such a thing? If you find yourself without a map, what other ways remain for you to get your bearings and set off on the course God desires?

In the absence of clear distinctions between these views, let me try to sketch out some of the more prevalent ideas about determining God's will and calling. I think that most Christians' statements about God's direction in their life would fit into one or more of these categories.

First, there are those who, when they talk about being called, seem to refer to a working of God's Spirit on their emotions, causing them to either desire or despise a certain course. Sometimes this means that they feel a sense of conviction, an inner burning or burden of the heart from which they seem unable to escape. (Some people even believe you must first try to escape from it!) At other times, people are waiting for a sense of peace about what they should do. They want consolation and reassurance that this is exactly where God is pointing them. Explanations given for decisions made in this way can degenerate into almost comically vague clichés. People begin to say things like, "Well, we're leaving this church because we've just sensed God moving our hearts away from this place." I gather that the thrust of such talk is to intimate that the speakers no longer have positive feelings when they think about their church family—a sensation that can only have a divine explanation, surely!

Then there's a group that searches for signs of confirmation that a given path is the one God wishes them to take. The required size and type of the sign are subject to personal taste.

Some want a strictly supernatural sign—something they can be sure could only have come from God Himself. Some simply want propitious circumstances. They speak often of God opening and closing doors. They testify that everything just falls into place when you're in line with God's will. Some find confirmation in seeming coincidences. A word spoken by a fellow believer, a song played on the radio, the pastor's preaching topic on Sunday or even a certain text of Scripture stumbled upon mentally or in their devotional reading. In sum, these believers feel it's wisest to wait to take a given path until they have some kind of guarantee from God that this is His will. By this measure, Gideon is to be commended for all that business with the fleece, as an exemplary believer who waited on God's confirmation, rather than as another example of man's sinful distaste for trusting God's promises!

A third kind of perspective wants nothing less than to hear the voice of God. The primary factor in decision making for these Christians is "God told me." While it would be natural to think of this view as being embraced most often by believers with charismatic leanings, as a Baptist I can bear witness that this perspective is no stranger to the other side of the aisle! Not long ago, I attended a one-day regional pastors' conference of a large cessationist denomination. It featured three speakers. All three of them, in the course of their respective sermons, made reference to an occasion where the voice of God spoke to them. So it seems that many within cessationist traditions are about as willing to say what God told them as any of our charismatic brothers. True, the means whereby we profess God spoke to us may differ. One side talks about God speaking to us via dreams and prophecies, while the other says we hear His voice inaudibly in our hearts. Nonetheless, the basic idea is the same: an extrabiblical revelation from God is the way to determine what we should do in a given situation.

Fortunately, there is a fourth sort of perspective that seems to have a growing awareness and acceptance among believers. And that is the view that might be called the 'blended' approach to God's will. It teaches that the will of God for a believer's life lies at the intersection of several important factors, including one's gifting, opportunities and desires, input from wise counsel, and maybe a couple others. In other words, you have to think about it! It's going to take some wisdom. For reasons we will discuss shortly, this approach seems vastly superior to the other decision-making strategies mentioned above. Unfortunately, I find that many believers who intellectually assent to the superiority of this strategy for finding God's calling still tend to slide into the vocabulary and methodology of the other views. That is, even though they believe that God's will is something that requires you to engage your intellect, they often continue to make decisions based on vague and mystical factors.

So not everyone means the same thing by God's calling. If you were to ask a group of modern Christians in the West, "Should I go as a disciple maker to a place less reached than where I find myself now?" you would likely meet with answers of all four types. Some will say, "Not until you are convicted about it." Others will say, "Not until you have some confirmation." Still others will say, "Not until God tells you to go." A few others will say, "Not until you've thought about it carefully." None of these approaches, however, are likely to result in your answering this question in the affirmative! It is very rare that a Christian, following these methods, arrives at the conclusion that he or she is called to be a missionary.

Finding What God Has Hidden

As we said above, this might tell us that God isn't calling many people. It might also tell us that we're looking for the wrong thing altogether! All four of these approaches are different ways of trying to discover the same thing: certainty about which path is the one God desires one to take. But what if this kind of certainty is something that God does not give? What if all quests to find the divinely-appointed course for our lives are vain? What if calling has no bearing on a Christian's wise decision making? This is precisely what I wish to argue. Below I will give seven reasons why the emphasis placed on finding God's calling is misguided and detrimental to the cause of missions.

1. It demands information God has withheld.

Theologians commonly make a distinction between God's revealed will and His secret will. Sometimes these are called His "will of precept" and His "will of decree." This does not mean that God has two different, schizophrenic wills that may be in conflict with one another. It simply means that God doesn't tell us everything that He intends to do in the world, but tells us what we need to know in order to obey Him (see Deut. 29:29). Some of His truth, some of His actions, some of His purposes are revealed to us in Scripture; and the rest are, well, a secret. There are some things He has not chosen to tell us. Will I be alive this time next year? Sorry, can't tell you. It's an unknowable secret!

It is vital that we think correctly about these aspects of God's will (as about all truths concerning God) for at least a couple reasons. First, thinking correctly about God's revealed will enables us to identify what we are actually accountable to do. When we stand at the crossroads of exportation, there are some things we can know and some things we will not know. We know (because He told us) that God wants us to work at bringing the gospel to the world. But only God knows, for He hasn't told us, what progress our generation will make in this regard—and that's okay! The only direction that we need to know in order to faithfully obey is His command.

God doesn't expect you to know His secret will. That's why it's a secret! God has revealed enough information in Scripture for you to make a decision about how to serve Him with your life. If there are billions of *unheards* in the world, you do not need to spend a lot of time fretting about which ones you should reach. The Great Commission establishes that Jesus wants Christians to go with the message to *unheards*. You are a Christian, therefore you may go. In other words, you do not need a special calling to decide to be a missionary, nor should you expect one!

Second, thinking correctly about God's secret will enables us to trust His providence. He will work all things out for good. This is one of the more peculiar idiosyncrasies of modern Christianity in the West. We worry far less about our sins messing up God's will than about our good intentions messing up God's will! I meet many young believers who seem to think God would be angered if they tried to be missionaries without a special call! How often have you heard someone say they feared their proactive obedience would get them "ahead of God"? As if such a thing were possible! You need not worry that you'll row so hard that God's boat will overturn! God's sovereign will is not a fragile thing to be broken by the likes of you or me. He will do what He has determined! So though I may not have a special revelation from God confirming my decision, I can throw myself into global disciple-making endeavors, confident that He is well-pleased by obedience to His revealed will.

2. It seeks guarantees where God offers none.

The hidden will of God leads us to an important conclusion: Christians do not know the future! Many of us seem to have gotten the opposite idea into our heads: that if we are walking with God and striving to obey Him, nothing should ever take us by surprise! We expect God to draw us a map of what is in our future, one that tells us where we are to go, what kind of work we should do, how we should do it, how long we should stay, etc. But we cannot know for sure what will take place even in the very near future (see James 4:13-16). He says all attempts to make plans without reserving for God the right to change them without notice are prideful. Why prideful? Because to do so is to fail to distinguish between what only God can know and what you as a human can know!

Here we see why many of the popular views of God's calling are so flawed. They profess to know about the future what cannot be known. I cannot tell you how many times I've heard students say something like, "I know that God wants me to change schools," or "I know that God wants me to marry Bill," or "I know that God wants me to pastor a church in the States." Do you know? Is it impossible for your application to be rejected, for your boyfriend to cheat on you or for you to die in a car accident this week? We frankly have very few guarantees about what may or may not happen in our lives. Yet one of the reasons so few Christians go is that they are waiting for just such a guarantee from God that their decision to become a missionary will lead to a blissful future.

The fact is that when I boarded a plane with my wife to come to China the first time, God had every right to allow it to crash into the ocean. He was free to allow us to be turned away at the border. He is free today to allow the police to be sent to my office to lock me up. At every fork in the path, at every cross-roads, we as believers can only say, "If God wills," and select a path to the best of our ability, relying on Him to bring us to His desired end. To throw around words like "know," "confirm" and "sure" is evidence of our prideful desire to know what God alone knows: the future. God does not give us as many guarantees about the outcomes of our decisions as we claim for ourselves. There are many factors that we should ponder as we make our decisions about the future: our opportunities, our abilities, our desires, our reasoning and our counsel. But all of those factors do not add up to a guarantee that taking a given path is going to have the outcome that we envision! Christians are not at liberty to carve their plans into stone, because God always reserves the right to change our course.

Believers who think of God's calling in this way are destined to forever live their lives on the path of least resistance. For whenever circumstances get rough, they immediately imagine that God disapproves of their course and proceed to steer into calmer waters. Unfortunately for the millions of *unheards* who need rescue, very few of them are adrift in calm waters! Where are believers to find the resolve necessary to endure persecution and suffering of every kind in order to bring the gospel to those without it?

3. It presumes to speak in God's place.

One of the most dangerous combinations of words in any language is the phrase "God told me." It is a truly unanswerable proposition, as it appeals to the highest authority in the universe. As many atheists would hasten to point out, many horrible things have been done in human history because of the potency of this phrase. The severe restrictions on this claim in the Bible show that they are fundamentally right in recognizing this danger (see Deut. 18:20; Jer. 23:9-40; Rev. 22:18-19; 2 Cor. 2:16-17). Unlike those atheists, God's people can have no desire to do away with all authoritative claims of revelation, but we must desire to restrict their use to those statements that truly did pass forth from the mouth of God.

That is why I find so alarming the alacrity with which believers are willing to say that God told them this or that. A couple years ago here in China, we hosted a wonderful nondenominational group of American students who placed a strong emphasis on discovering God's will for their future. As I talked to each of them in turn over the course of their trip, I was astounded to hear them speak so confidently and in such detail about God's opinions lately made known to them! One of them told us, "I had thought God wanted me to go to that country, but later He told me that He had just wanted me to be willing to go there." Such talk was typical. For the record, these divulgences from God were not made via a charismatic experience, but simply by a vague impression on their hearts.

On one level, such uncontrolled speculations on the secret will of God are just humorous. I never cease to derive amusement from the clever one-liners and zingers attributed to God by creative preachers who enjoy make-believing that God talks like a sassy Waffle House waitress! Yet on another level, they're serious and frightening. To talk with a straight face about what God said when His voice has not been audibly heard is to seriously depersonalize God and treat Him, well, like we treat our imaginations! Would you be comfortable putting words in the mouth of any person you know? Would you feel free to quote them as saying something when you haven't heard the words right out of their mouths? Of course not, because they're "real" people. The fact that God is invisible, spiritual and supernatural should not lead us to the conclusion that we are free to imagine His whisperings in every stirring of our heart! On the contrary, the eternal value of every word that has truly come from God should make us tremble at the audacity that compares what we have to say with what He has to say!

4. It is naïve about its own bias.

It is never very surprising what believers decide is the perfect will of God for their lives. Have you ever met a teenage boy who thought a girl was "the one" foreordained to be with him, even though he was personally repulsed by her? Not likely. Not much changes with our decisions later in life, either. I know that it is all too easy for me personally to confuse the will of God for me with the will of me for me! When we're talking about whether or not you should be exported to an area of greater need, you must admit that there are only about a hundred or so subconscious reasons to fool yourself into believing that God is against you going as a missionary. As was discussed in a previous chapter, we should be suspicious of our own desires to avoid the dangers and deprivations that lie down the road of missions.

Even when someone has started down the path of exportation, it is still not a sure thing he will end up exported to a place with a high factor of Great Commission need. Our biases pose a major threat here, as well. Every year, more missionaries are exported to places where there are not a large number of *unheards*, and sometimes not even a large number of people! I know a family who were endeavoring to go as missionaries to an incredibly remote Arctic environment where very few people lived and where a gospel-preaching church already existed. They thought it was so neat that God had called them to such a barren wilderness, since they'd always been really into outdoor activities as a family. There's a word for that kind of enchantment: naiveté. Others are so excited that God has called them to go to the country of their ancestors to preach the gospel. Such desires are driven more by fond memories of Grandma's cooking than they are by the Great Commission directive. Of course, I'm sure we've all heard people joke about being called to the Bahamas or Hawaii. But the jokes have a sharp edge: people have desires of their own creation, and it's easy to repackage them as God's calling on your life.

So before you write off the possibility of becoming a missionary, please consider that what you heard as the call of God may sound strangely like your own thoughts. We as Christians must expect that the most God-glorifying plan for our lives will in fact be the path of self-denial, not the path that gratifies all our fondest wishes.

5. It denies responsibility for our actions.

One of the reasons that the language of God's call appeals to us in our decision making is that it seems to exempt us from all further examinations. After all, what can you say to someone when they tell you that God has called them to do something? Not much, besides praise their obedience! Now, I'm not so cynical as to say that this normally happens on a conscious level, as if many believers are lying about their feelings to escape accountability. But we soon discover intuitively that when we say that God has called us, many brothers and sisters in Christ will stop questioning the wisdom of our decision.

More gravely, when we try to claim our current actions as our response to God's call or the absence thereof, it is in a way denying all responsibility for the outcome of the choice. If

God didn't tell me to go to the mission field, I certainly can't be blamed for those *unheards'* inability to hear the gospel! However, as we said above, God expects us to make the best choices with the information that He has given us. If the Great Commission sends believers to the world, we have no reason to think that He should have to give more information before we think we are responsible to go!

If you don't want to be a missionary, say so. There are even good reasons to not go, as we have seen, but own up to your decisions. Don't blame God if you are a largely ineffective disciple maker. Don't say that He didn't give you enough reason to think you should go to the world. Don't pretend you were as willing as anyone to go, but God unfairly held you back! He has given you the freedom to go and the responsibility to consider going. Whether you do or not is on you.

6. It ignores the proper bases for our decisions.

Above we talked about a superior form of decision making, one that weighs important factors and then searches for the right thing to do. As we said, too often this approach is used as yet another tool for discovering God's "perfect will" or His calling. As I hope is evident by now, the quest itself is vain. It is searching for something that God is not in the habit of giving. I do believe that though the quest is in error, the tool is right and often yields positive results.

Imagine that you are brought to the foot of a mountain, given a shovel and told to dig a tunnel through to the other side of the mountain. Your tool is the shovel. Your goal is to get through to the other side of the mountain. But supposing that, as you dig, you get it into your head that there exists only one right way to burrow through the soil and rock. Now you're looking for something that doesn't exist, but your tool is still good, and much good will be done if you continue digging forward, even though your understanding of the work is flawed. This is something like what I mean when I say the tool—wise consideration—is good, though I do not believe that anyone is going to use it to find the yellow brick road leading to God's perfect will.

This sixth reason indicates another, much more serious error. It is forgetting the tool altogether! What I mean by this is that some Christians, having settled upon some mystical strategy for hearing God's call or finding His perfect will, overlook the tool that is most effective in leading us to accomplish our mission. That tool, again, is wise consideration of multiple factors: God's revealed will in Scripture, our own abilities and circumstances, the *unheard* factor in our current locale, the strength of the church in our current locale, the input of godly counsel, etc. When a Christian resolves to make his life's decisions based on a wise weighing of factors such as these, he will end up on a truly radical path. The path hit upon in this way is the one most likely to carry him to the world's unreached ones. Meanwhile, abandoning these God-appointed guides in his decision making is necessarily to base his plans on something inferior. Without the shovel, there is much less hope indeed of emerging on the other side of the mountain!

To ignore the right bases for our decision making is, in most cases, to ensure that we will not take the best path. God has provided for us the information we need to make wise decisions that contribute to the accomplishment of our mission. If we as Christians don't have enough wisdom to make a decision, we need only ask God for more (see James 1:5)!

Ironically, the Christian who thinks carefully about his path will make far more radical choices than the Christian who is driven by what seem to be more radical decision-making methods! While the former is likely to discover the utter reasonableness of God's demands on his life, the latter is likely to mistake his own voice for God's and make something mystical out of a very ordinary desire.

7. It kills proactive obedience.

If I believe that there is a yellow brick road to be followed and all the other roads are not God's will, you may be sure that I will pitch a tent at that crossroads until I'm dead sure which way is right! Sadly, I believe this is happening in churches in largely-reached areas all over the world. Believers aren't sure that God wants them to be missionaries, so they don't dare go down that path. This idea that we should wait on God's confirming direction for our every move and decision takes away from the glory of being the representatives of Christ on this earth! He has pointed us in the direction of the world. He has promised His presence and authority will never be taken from us. Then he says, "Go!" No more specifics. That's for us to work on. What an immense and glorious responsibility!

You say, "God, can I go to Africa?" He says, "Go!"

You say, "God, how about India? Can I go there?" He says, "Go!"

You say, "But God, what about the unreached in Brazil?" He says, "Go!"

He is for us. He is behind us. He is before us. He is with us. He is within us. But He lets us choose where to go! Of course, He will providentially guide and direct us into His secret will. That doesn't diminish by one iota the grand privilege we have of truly, actually doing something for God on this planet! To continually yank back on the reins and look to God for confirmation betrays our lack of faith in His Word. What more do we need that He could not promise us in the Great Commission? If you believe He is with you, launch out toward the world in glorious proactive obedience and watch God's hand work through you!

This is the kind of obedience that characterizes the missionaries in the book of Acts. Let's go back and visit Philip again for a minute. There are three episodes in Philip's story that tell us about his evangelistic efforts: to the Samaritans (see Acts 8:4-8), to the Ethiopian eunuch (see 8:26-39), and to the region between Azotus and Caesarea (see 8:40). In each case, Philip comes upon his preaching targets in a different way. What is Philip doing in Samaria? His arrival there seems to be related to the persecution by Saul in Jerusalem, which apparently has caused him (and many other believers) to seek for a place where they are in less danger (see 8:1-4). Philip goes to Samaria and, apparently without any special divine compulsion, preaches the gospel (see 8:5). What about the eunuch? In this case, there is a special revelation from an angel to Philip telling him to move in a certain direction (see 8:26). Philip obediently responds to this call, which is followed up by the Spirit's direct instruction to go to the eunuch's chariot (see 8:29). Interestingly enough, the Spirit doesn't find it necessary to tell Philip what to do once he's in the chariot! And third, how does Philip "find himself" in Azotus? The details are unclear, but it looks like some kind of teleportation that modern missionaries would envy (see 8:39)! Again, Philip looks around, sees that he's in a place that needs the gospel, and, without any evidence of a call, begins to preach (see 8:40).

While it is self-evident that all three cases are equally a part of God's plan for Philip, it is also clear that one of these cases gets all the press! Most often, when a believer talks about hearing God's call to become a missionary, they are thinking of something resembling Philip's second episode. They want audible confirmation directing them to a geographical area. What I would ask you to notice here is that all three of these episodes are examples of legitimate decision making. The common thread in these episodes is Philip's commitment to preach the gospel, not the manner in which he decides to whom he will preach.

Compare this with the average Christian in modern times. We believe that it is only our responsibility to preach Christ to *unheards* when we have been specially interrupted by God and directed to a particular place. Philip, however, was proactively preaching to *unheards* before God sent him to the eunuch! Moreover, Philip continued preaching to *unheards* after his mission to the eunuch was complete—all the way until the curtain falls!

So how does Philip answer the question, "Which unbelievers am I supposed to preach to?" It seems that his answer is "any and all." Philip never has the safety on. His finger is always on the trigger. If he sees an *unheard*, he is going to preach. If he doesn't see an *unheard*, he's not going to climb into a tree stand and wait. He's going to go track them down.

For brevity's sake, I will not prolong this section to consider the decision making of Paul, the other apostles or other Christians featured in the New Testament. Though among their decision making factors you will find special revelatory experience, propitious circumstances and apparent coincidence, you will find none of the idea that our mission to preach Christ to *unheards* can only begin when we've had a special calling. The Great Commission is enough to take the exported path. I do not deny that once we are moving on that path, God may from time to time direct us supernaturally to specific *unheards*, just as he directed Philip. However, you need never wait on him to do so. Just start moving. He interrupts Philip when He wants him to reach the eunuch. He stops Paul when He wants him in Macedonia. And He'll direct your path to those people that He wants you to reach, too.

Shifting to a Volunteer Mind-Set

So, have we gotten anywhere? I hope so. Let's review for a second. God's will for our lives is not a yellow brick road that He reveals to us. He does not tell us what we are supposed to do in most of the nonmoral decisions in our lives. So there is no reason to wait on making a decision until you have this kind of divine confirmation. In place of this step-by-step instruction, Jesus left us with a macrogoal: preach the gospel to the world. This means we can humbly, yet boldly, exercise our God-given power to proactively make wise decisions that help us achieve that end, and then own up to our own responsibility when it turns out we made a poor one. Only God makes perfectly wise decisions at every possible crossroads. When we find that we have decided foolishly (i.e., out of line with the macrogoal Jesus assigned us), we need not fear that we have unleashed a chain-reaction butterfly effect that will prevent us from ever glorifying God again. Instead, we recognize that His wise and glorious path factored in our foolish one! Trusting God's wise providence in this way, we are empowered to go back to digging at the mountain in front of us toward the end that He has commanded us to pursue.

Let's bring this down to the exact intersection that this book is most interested in: Should you become an exported missionary? Should you be one of those who choose to leave their own largely-reached area to go to a place where the *unheards* are in abundance? Most Christians decide to answer "no." I pray you will consider more carefully. God has given us a macrogoal, a megavision for disciple making. If you could reach into your brain, switch off all your biases, deactivate all your notions of God's calling and enter in the data of the world's condition, what would be the wisest, most natural thing for you to do? The point of this chapter is simply this: you are free and responsible to volunteer to go wherever you can be of maximum effectiveness in making disciples. If God has commanded us in His Word to do something, then it is never wrong for us to do that thing!

Though occasionally I meet a missionary who feels that he was beaten and compelled Jonah-style by God, the majority were overjoyed to be able to join such an illustrious endeavor—even the ones who believed they were called! The history of Christian missions is full of the stories of men who saw the glory of the mission and freely offered their lives to go. There is absolutely no harm in your volunteering. Do you fear God is unable to stop you if He really wants you somewhere else?

People often ask me when God called me to go as a missionary to northeast China. I used to feel pressure to provide them with a date, an experience, a story—anything other than, "Well, my mentor thought this was a needy area, so I came." Now, when people ask me, I try to remember to tell them, "Let's see . . . God called me about forty days after Easter—almost two thousand years ago!" The Great Commission is all the call that you or I need to begin our movement toward the world. He will direct your steps—you need not worry about that. I'd be more worried about Him directing your sitting!

If our churches in the West would begin to change their emphasis from God's calling to our volunteering, I believe that a great number of believers would be released to make disciples around the world. Quickly and finally, here are a couple of the positive effects to be gained from this emphasis shift.

First, it gives believers permission to obey the Great Commission. There are many missions-loving Christians who have already decided disappointedly that they are not called to be missionaries. If someone would clear their vision in this area, they might find the path to the world wide-open in front of them and rush forward rejoicing! When a preacher tells a church about his experience of God's calling, he is adding boulders to the dam. He is teaching believers, though perhaps unintentionally, that they should stay put until they have a similar experience. On the other hand, when we help God's people to think correctly about His will, the dam will break up and the dry valley will be watered.

Second, it allows us to stop sending the unqualified. Many missions organizations and churches send and support missionaries not because they believe that the candidate's field is a needy one or that the candidate is especially qualified, but because the candidate professes to be called! One elderly member of a mission board that I know often imparts this nugget to groups of young missionary candidates: "You won't stay on the mission field unless you're called." Which means he is far more interested in a candidate's call than in his training. Nor will he be very anxious to analyze why missionaries from his board come off the field. It's obvious to him—they're not called!

Changing the emphasis, however, allows us to trump their trump! When a young person in your ministry tells you that God has called him to do something harebrained, you can tell him confidently that God has called him to do no such thing! Not because the thing is so foolish (good luck convincing him of that, anyway), but because that's not the way God's call works. You can lovingly direct believers into wiser, more effective decision making.

Third, it calls on all to consider their own place of service. No one can safely set his life on autopilot. There is always the possibility that we should move to another place. I cannot say that God has called me to stay in this Chinese city until the day I die, no matter how much I may hope that He will allow me that privilege. He may have a totally different future in store. It may be a future that He will providentially allow to fall upon me; or it may be that as I continue to measure my effectiveness as a disciple maker in this place, I will one day discover that the Great Commission goal calls me on to another place. Either way, every believer must be challenged constantly to consider their path carefully.

The truth is, we don't only go through the "stay or go" cross-roads once in our lives. The mission paradigm means that our eyes are always forward on the mission, on the evangelization of the world. Again and again, we must ask ourselves if there is enough disciple-making work around us to merit our choosing the "stay" path. Having shed ourselves of extrabiblical ideas of God's will, we must forever remain volunteers, time and again willing to do whatever is most expedient for the accomplishment of the mission.

10

Off Deeds, Onto Words

Are ministries of mercy part of the church's global mission?

Have you ever tried to find your state or province on a map that doesn't have the borders drawn for you? Several times I've had Chinese people ask me to show them on a world map where my hometown is located. I never have too much trouble with this request. I find the Great Lakes, head south a bit, find Cincinnati, and jab at a spot half a centimeter or so above it. That's where I'm from. But supposing that the inquirer didn't just want to know where Ohio is, but wanted to know exactly where Ohio isn't—in other words, where the borders of Ohio lie? That would be a tad more difficult. I know that Cincinnati is in the southwest corner. I know for sure that if you cross over the Ohio River, you are officially in a fearsome land known as "Kentucky." There's Lake Erie to the north, so that one's not too hard, either. But the state lines on the east and west, though straight as an arrow, would be hard to pinpoint accurately.

I have no problem identifying locations that are most definitely within the borders of Ohio. It's also easy for me to show you hundreds of places I know are without a doubt not part of

Ohio. But there are a couple tricky points on the map where I could do little better than guess.

While you may be more familiar with your home state's borders than I (I hear you Hawaiians snickering), I think that many Christians have a similar difficulty when it comes to identifying what is and what is not gospel ministry. What is and what is not the work that the church is to be doing in this age? Sure, there are some things that we don't even have to ponder; we know they're part of the mission. Sharing the gospel with unbelievers. Establishing churches in areas where there are none. Discipling new converts. There are also some activities that are clearly not gospel ministry, and no one seems to argue that they are. But then there's a murky in-between region where we seem to lose our bearings. Some seem to think these activities are true gospel ministry; others insist that they are not. There don't seem to be clear signs informing us that we've left the state. How then do we go about deciding if these activities are related to our mission?

Somewhere in this foggy area is what we sometimes call "justice ministry" or "mercy ministry." These works are those that Christians do to demonstrate God's love by acting for the benefit of others, especially the poor and needy. This type of ministry is normally distinguished from "proclamation ministry," whereby the gospel is declared to those who do not believe it. Some prefer to say that the latter is a ministry of words while the former is a ministry of deeds. Many find it helpful to say that these two kinds of ministries together form the church's mission to the world. Others aren't sure. Are we still in Ohio or did we cross a border?

What we know for sure is that this world is experiencing a dire shortage of mercy. There are orphans living on the streets. There are survivors of natural disasters who are now homeless.

There are starving masses and villages without clean drinking water. There are those afflicted with painful illnesses, lacking the most basic medical care. There are victims of human trafficking, the drug trade and unjust wars. Add to these the less sensational but equally tragic effects of abortion, addictions and abuse, and you're left with a broken world indeed. There can be no question concerning what Christians are to feel about such ingrained evil in our world. There is, however, a question about what we are to do about these needs, and how it relates to the need of unbelievers to hear the gospel.

In this chapter, I want to try to show that while acts of mercy and justice are indispensable parts of the Christian life, they may not fall within the borders of the church's primary mission in this age. Believers and churches should attempt to think of their mission as proclaiming the gospel and, whenever they can along the path of proclamation, alleviating physical suffering. But some believers today think the reverse is true: that their essential calling is being a force of mercy and justice and, whenever they are able along that path, proclaiming the gospel. In other words, at times mercy ministry can be controlling; proclamation ministry seems to be squeezed in.

What does this have to do with a book about missions? It is imperative that we identify the borders of gospel ministry and the church's mission, because it makes a big impact on our churches' exporting capacity. That is to say, as our churches' emphasis seems to shift from proclamation ministry to deeds ministry, the motivation behind missions can be drained. Can we expect men and women to take radical steps toward obeying the global disciple making when an emphasis on this other kind of ministry competes with it? To answer this question, we need to start at the foundation.

Why Words Are Necessary

Older Christian leaders who have seen more than a couple waves and trends in recent church history seem to concur that there has been a renewed interest in and pursuit of proclamation ministry in recent years. I, for one, am exceedingly grateful for many advocates of proclamation ministry who have used all their influence to convince young men of the necessity of preaching. They have shown in teaching and writing, far more clearly than I could, why the nature of the gospel makes us into proclaimers. Many young preachers have been energized by this emphasis and are entering pulpits with a passionate resolve to sow the life-giving seed of the Word.

This is a welcome change from a trend that continues in many churches today—swinging away from proclamation ministry and toward a view of deeds that renders words superfluous. The favorite slogan that accompanies this misguided campaign has been "Preach the gospel. Use words if necessary." (One of those phrases that ends up being attributed to everyone from Ronald Reagan to Ronald McDonald.) Their meaning, of course, is that we Christians have all kinds of things to be doing in the world besides the verbal communication of the gospel, and if we would just be faithful in doing those things, then our proclamation ministry might actually start to do some good. They insist that without a foundation of good works, our preaching is just so much racket.

This trend recognizes rightly that there is certainly a need for Christian proclamation to be accompanied by holy living, and it is very wise to point out that our good works are a powerful argument for the truth of the gospel. But very often, this campaign overshoots the mark and begins to prioritize good works in the place of gospel proclamation. That is, less effort and fewer resources go into speaking the message of the gospel to others, and more effort and resources are channeled into activities that the world will recognize as praiseworthy. At its most extreme, advocates of this view may give the impression that our works are sufficient in themselves to fulfill our mission, as if unbelievers would be converted just by witnessing Christians not cheating on our wives or taxes or golf scores.

To put it plainly, the gospel must be communicated with words! There is no giving the gospel without using this medium! Why? The gospel is a message. It is news. It is a report, a testimony about something that has happened in the past. While you can use your deeds to show people that you love them, that you are a just person or even that you have experienced mercy yourself, you cannot use your deeds to show people that Jesus was God in human flesh or that He died on a cross to pay for their sin debt.

As I said, these points have been made so well by others that I hesitate to say much here. Realize, though, how important it is to remember that the gospel is about something that has happened in the past. A missionary friend of mine not long ago e-mailed our team a picture of his own face with a pronounced black eye as well as some other scrapes and bruises. There was no title to the e-mail and there were no words in the body. Naturally, it was only a couple seconds before someone wrote back and asked what in the world had happened to him. He informed us that he had just been beaten and robbed road-to-Jericho style. (Ironically, while on a furlough in the States!) While it's true that we had already seen the transformative results of his encounter with criminals, his picture alone did not and could not tell us what had happened to him. Words were required to communicate the content of the past event to us.

Now suppose that my friend subscribed to a particular life philosophy that said, "Tell your friends what happens in your life. Use words if necessary." Maybe, based on my friend's emotional cues, the appearance of his wounds and his subsequent hesitancy about going to a downtown area after dark, I could piece together what went down on that night. This kind of deduction would only get me so far, however. I could not find out, for example, what his attackers looked like, how many there were, why they attacked him, if he provoked them, how long the attack lasted, if anyone intervened or if he was likely to be attacked again! While I might find out that he had in fact been mugged, I would remain completely in the dark about the mugging's significance, the meaning behind it.

The gospel is not only a message about something that happened; it is also a message about what that event means for the hearers. The significance of any definite event that occurred in the past cannot be communicated without verbal explanation. This is why the Bible depicts the apostles "proclaiming Christ" to the same people who had called for His crucifixion. These Jerusalem crowds knew many of the facts framing the message, but proclamation was still necessary to make clear the significance of the events for them. It still remained to proclaim repentance and forgiveness of sins in the name of the Crucified One.

So because the gospel is news about something that happened in the past which has immense significance to every individual on the earth, gospel ministry must deal primarily in words. Unbelievers, by the unaided observation of many good deeds, are unlikely to learn the facts of Christ's atonement and are completely unable to ascertain its significance for them. This is not to say that the lifestyle that we exhibit to the world is inconsequential. Our deeds certainly have the ability to either corroborate or undermine our verbal testimony. It is to say that Chinese people in the city where I live will not believe the gospel without proclaimers of the gospel. Gospel ministry cannot be done without proclamation.

The Importance of Being Just

If you're reading this book, it's unlikely that you subscribe to the school of thought that disregards proclamation ministry. I mention that trend only to affirm by contradiction that proclamation ministry is essential and irreplaceable, and you probably didn't have many doubts about that. Like I said at the opening of this chapter, we don't have too much trouble saying that proclamation ministry is clearly a part of gospel ministry. The problem is that we also want to affirm that deeds are important. I certainly don't want to be read as saying that there is no need for Christians to perform works of loving mercy and justice in the world! The question is, are we still in Ohio? Is this still part of the church's mission on the earth?

As with several other issues that have already come across our path in these pages, it is necessary to clarify that my intention is in no way to deny the responsibility of God's people to be a force of justice and mercy in the world. But if we have a responsibility to act justly, isn't that the same as having a mission to act justly? How can it be simultaneously maintained that Christians have a responsibility to be a force of mercy and that this is not the church's mission? The distinction seems to hinge on the not-terribly-obvious difference between the concepts of "the Christian's responsibility" and "the church's mission." Let's see if we can't distinguish between the two, and then we'll see if the Bible supports such a distinction.

First of all, what do we mean when we say the "Christian's responsibility"? Our responsibilities are the multitudinous answers to the question, "What kinds of things are Christians supposed to do?" This includes the whole of the process of our sanctification, whereby the children of God are effectively yet incompletely molded into the image of Christ in this life. So anything that we as Christians are instructed in the Bible to do or not to do is a real duty that we must be careful to fulfill. For example, I am to be a loving husband to my wife. To fail to do so is to neglect my responsibility of living out the gospel in my marriage. Some other examples: I am to speak truthfully to others. I am to be a giver. I am to have a diligent work ethic. And, as we are talking about in this chapter, I am to be a merciful agent of justice, doing good deeds for others. These—and many others—are all my responsibilities as a child of God. Wherever I discover a discrepancy between the person of Jesus of Christ and the person of me, I must rise to action to resolve it—and there are many discrepancies!

Let's take another look at that responsibility to be an agent of justice. I am to do good to all men. I am to demonstrate to undeserving people the mercy of God. I am to let justice govern my actions. I am to sacrifice my material goods to meet the needs of others. As John wrote in his first epistle, how can we say that we have experienced the love of God if we neglect to meet material needs when we encounter them (see 1 John 3:17)? I am in a city in China that has no lack of poor people. There are many times that my wife and I come face-to-face with real, desperate material needs. I must remember in such times that I have a responsibility to sacrifice my own resources to remedy such needs. The gospel leads us to do no less.

But how are these responsibilities any different from "the church's mission"? The Christian's responsibilities seem to cover all the bases—all aspects of our personal sanctification. The church's mission, however, describes what our corporate work in this world in this age is like. The church's mission is the single answer to the question, "To what end is the church corporately working on this earth?" That end, as we have seen repeatedly, is the propagation of the gospel throughout the entire world population. So as the body of Christ in a particular place, when we consider what our work should be toward the world, we must be thinking in disciple-making terms. The church's work toward the world is not political, medical, economic, environmental or educational. It is proclamational.

To clear up possible misunderstandings, the church's mission has at least two distinctions from the believer's responsibilities. First, it is corporate, while your sanctification is personal. For example, you are personally commanded to love your own neighbor as your own self. Obedience to that command rises and falls on you. Every other believer around you could fail in this regard, and you could still faithfully obey. In other words, this is an individual command. I am arguing that the biblical commands for Christians to mercifully care for the needy fall into the same category. This is not to say that the church does not equip and assist you in fulfilling this or any other obligation that lies along the path of personal sanctification, but it's to say that the church is indirectly involved. The Great Commission, on the other hand, is not an individual command. No one believer—or even one particular church—is going to complete this task singlehandedly! It is understood that it is a task that the global church across the centuries is going to work on jointly, though of course (as with any corporate task) there will be specific tasks for every individual to accomplish.

Second, the church's mission is a time-sensitive commission, not merely a timeless duty. Mentally compare, for a moment, the work of world evangelization with the work of ministering to the needy as they both relate to the whole of biblical history. Who, in the panorama of the Bible's story, was responsible to show mercy to the poor and needy? The answer seems obvious. The Old Testament made clear that God's covenant people were to be characterized by their mercy and justice towards others (see Exod. 22:22-27; Lev. 25:25-55; Deut. 24:14-22; Ps. 109:6-20; Mic. 6:8). In the prophetic books, judgment was announced against nations—both Jewish and Gentile—for their failure to show mercy toward the disadvantaged (see Ezek. 22:23-29; Dan. 4:27). Jesus lambasted the scribes and Pharisees for their hypocrisy in literal obedience to laws like tithing while blatantly disregarding the point for which those laws were given—that mercy would be shown to the poor (see Matt. 23:23). So it is not a surprise at all that Christians under the new covenant Christ establishes are also to be lovers of mercy (see Matt. 5:7; 1 Tim. 6:18; James 3:17). Compassion is integrally related to holiness, as it springs out of God's very nature (see Luke 6:36). All humans in every age have had the responsibility before God to do good deeds for others. But a commission like the one we have received to preach the gospel is a bit more time-sensitive, isn't it? Unlike Abraham's family, Moses' wilderness people, Joshua's conquering nation, David's glorious kingdom or Nehemiah's rebuilding remnant, God's people in this age have been uniquely entrusted with a particular task: to glorify God by making disciples of the nations. That is not to say that God's people in the Old Testament did not desire or pursue the worldwide glorification of God, only to say that they were not prescribed this exact work by which to glorify God (see Exod. 7:1-5; 1 Sam. 17:45-

47; 1 Kings 8:10-13). This mission is uniquely for us in this age (see Eph. 3:8-11).

So how do our individual responsibilities and our corporate mission relate to each other? For starters, involvement with the church is one of our responsibilities as individual believers. Fellowship with and service in a church are among those things that Christians are supposed to do. Therefore, the mission of the church toward the world must necessarily be a prominent feature of our individual lives, as has been discussed earlier in this book. Because we are in a church, we must be involved in her mission of making disciples. Additionally, unless we are personally making advances on the sanctification front, we will find our involvement with the mission to be feeble and lackluster. Without personal holiness, our witness to the lost world will lack persuasiveness. Any facet of our lives, including our relationship to those in need, when burnished by contact with the gospel, becomes a glowing testament to the saving power of God.

I have tried to show that, contrary to the dual nature of the church's mission proposed by many, the church's mission to preach the gospel to the nations belongs in a separate category from its members' individual commitments to show mercy to the needy. Now, can this distinction between the believer's individual responsibilities and the church's corporate mission be supported biblically? I think so.

Mercy in the New Testament

Some Christians who are passionate about works of mercy and justice are very eager to demonstrate biblically that the church has an obligation to perform these kinds of ministries. But it seems to others, myself included, that many of the New Testament passages that are often touted as examples of mercy ministries seem a little strained. There seem to be some important differences between the orientation of the early church and the kind of commitment being proposed by mercy ministry advocates. In the teaching of Jesus, the example of Acts and the instruction of the Epistles, it is unquestionable that the New Testament commends acts of mercy and justice. This does not necessarily mean that these passages are teaching that the church relates to the work of ministering to the needy in the same way as preaching to *unheards*. Let me try to point out a few of those differences and why they seem to reinforce the unique priority of the Commission.

First, notice that in many of the examples of mercy ministry in the Bible, the beneficiaries are believing brothers and sisters. It is true that we see radical generosity in the early church. People are selling their property to meet material needs (see Acts 2:45; 4:32-35). The church also is committed to care for the widows in their number (see 6:1-3). The apostle Paul expects the churches he has planted to contribute financially to alleviating dire poverty in Judea (see Rom. 15:25-27). Do these examples not give mercy ministries a strong biblical precedent? Yes and no. In all of the cases mentioned above, it is clearly other believers who are receiving the benefits of the generosity. We are here still a great distance away from the idea of churches working to make the unbelieving world a better place! There is clearly preferential treatment given to the household of faith (see Gal. 6:10). This is not at all what we would expect to find if mercy ministry was, like Great Commission ministry, a foundational part of the church's mission toward the world.

Second, we do not see the church in Acts or its leaders in the Epistles making a priority of the advancement of mercy and justice in the world. If the early church was committed to such,

Luke was strangely silent about it. The book of the Acts of the Apostles is, after all, largely an account of how the message of the gospel radiated outward from Jerusalem and toward the world (see Acts 1:8; 28:31). In all of the apostles' endeavors, it is rare indeed that Luke mentions anything that could be construed as what we think of today as mercy ministry. Again, this is not to say that individual Christians in the churches springing up all over the ancient world were not living lives of radical generosity and justice. It is only to point out that we do not see the church corporately mobilizing its manpower and resources to address these needs in the world. Let us not forget that the Roman world of that day was every bit as dark and depraved as ours. The streets of the cities where Paul ministered were the sites of injustice and suffering that modern people do not easily comprehend.[24]

It may be argued that we read about Great Commission ministry in Acts because this was Paul and the other apostles' unique calling. There may have been thriving ministries of mercy toward outsiders in the churches the apostles planted, but that is pure speculation. In Acts, when it comes to those outside the church, the mercy we see the apostles concerned about is the mercy of God shown through the cross. We certainly have trouble finding support for the idea of the church leading a large-scale campaign against injustice in the world.

Third, many of the supposed examples of mercy ministry in the Bible are miracles. Jesus outdid every man who has ever lived in showing mercy to needy men. But the stories are all about His miraculous works (see Matt. 14:14; 20:29-34; Acts 10:38). Peter and Paul are often credited for their merciful works in the book of Acts, as well as miracles (see Acts 3:1-9; 14:8-10). This doesn't mean that their mercy doesn't count. Those who were healed certainly wouldn't think so! It does mean that we can't draw too straight of a line between what they did and what we are going to do.

For example, Paul once exorcised a demon from a slave girl who was being used by her owners as a fortune-teller (see Acts 16:16-18). We might reason, "Well, Paul cast demons out of a girl who was being exploited economically, therefore we need to minister on behalf of those who are being exploited economically in our day." But this is a bit simplistic. One need only observe Paul's attitude in this situation to see that it's not quite the same thing. Paul hasn't exactly made a priority out of helping the girl, nor does he seem motivated to rescue her from her economic plight (see 16:18)!

Nevertheless, Christians should act mercifully. If you have the power to work miracles, as the apostles sometimes did, then it seems you should utilize that power on behalf of the needy. But this makes their seeming lack of emphasis on such ministry all the more striking! They were gifted in a way that allowed them to alleviate suffering in such a powerful way, yet they apparently had other things on their minds. This means that it is far from clear that the miracles of mercy in the New Testament instruct the nonapostolic modern church to prioritize care for the needy.

Also, it is important that we remember that many of Jesus' miracles were not displays of mercy alone, any more than they were displays of power alone. It is clear that His mighty works entailed additional purposes, such as to serve as signs and instruction to the observers (see Mark 6:51-52; John 14:11). A missionary friend working in a rather primitive environment told me once that he thought our missions efforts should submit to the pattern of Jesus: first addressing the material needs of a community, then addressing the spiritual. While this thinking sounds very tidy, it is not apparent that Jesus by his miracle-working is establishing a pattern for the gospel ministry (Paul certainly didn't seem to think so)—the timing and setting of His miracles is far too varied to be sure that Jesus thought meeting material needs to be preparatory to believing in Him (see Mark 6:32-44). In fact, His explicit statements about miracles flat out deny it (see Luke 11:29)! So though we can be sure that Jesus was showing mercy, it is not a sure thing that He is establishing a pattern of ministry for His church.

Again, Jesus commanding a man to stretch out his hand to be instantly made whole and a Christian nurse coaching a man through physical therapy to possibly regain use of his legs are not really the same thing (see Mark 3:5). When we are dealing with miracles, we are talking about something that the majority of us readily admit we cannot do. True, Jesus sent His disciples on their preaching tour with instructions to serve the needy (see Matt. 10:1-8). He also empowered them with miraculous power to do so. The fact that He has not given you that power should make you think twice before you decide He's sent you forth in the same way as them!

A fourth difference concerns the personal acts of mercy that are abundant in the New Testament. Above, I said that there is a lack of organizational priority on meeting physical or material needs in the early church. Here I want to take another risky step forward and say that we don't even see much of a personal prioritization of mercy ministry by Christians in the early church record. Though we do see Christians acting in love and mercy, we do not see the kind of proactive search for the needy that we would expect to see if these kinds of mercy were integral to our mission. Let's assess one well-known illustration of mercy, the parable of the good Samaritan (see Luke 10:25-37). In Jesus' story, a man traveling the dangerous road from Jerusalem to Jericho is ambushed by robbers and left for dead (see Luke 10:30). Though a priest and a Levite pass by him without helping, a despised Samaritan mercifully responds to his need and rescues him (see 10:31-33). Here we see a man giving sacrificially, allowing the needs of another to become a drain on his budget, schedule and safety (see 10:34-35). But what we don't see is a man on this road looking for people who have been left half-dead. He is not proactive—he happens upon this situation. Unlike the priest and the Levite who choose to ignore the suffering that is in their path, the Samaritan is commended for stopping to help. The Good Samaritan doesn't stop because he's in the good Samaritan ministry, but because this is the compassionate thing to do!

Similarly, the apostle Paul says that we are to do good to all men as we are given the opportunity (see Gal. 6:10). Now, what exactly it means to have opportunity is debated. Clearly, Paul can't be talking about helping people when it won't cost us anything. None of us would ever really be responsible to show mercy then. I think it makes good sense to hear Paul setting a similar scene for our mercy as we see in the parable of the good Samaritan. It was certainly inconvenient, dangerous and expensive for the Samaritan to help the Jericho road victim, but he still saw himself as "having opportunity"! So Paul seems to be saying that as we are presented with opportunities for serving those in need, we should be quick to respond in sacrificial love. However you read it, what I really want us to notice is how inconceivable it would be for Paul to say something like this about the gospel ministry! Can you imagine Paul saying, "As we have opportunity, let us preach the gospel to all men"? Paul's whole life was about making opportunities to preach the gospel! There is clearly a distinction between these kinds of works in his mind.

Fifth and last, the vision of the world toward which the early church labored is substantially different from the alternative vision that a prioritization of mercy ministry creates. Mercy ministry advocates often give the impression that the church's mission is to strive to make our communities and, in turn, our world, more just. This vision has an optimistic overtone. We are anticipating the church becoming an increasingly influential force of mercy and compassion in the world. This vision seems to be at odds with the one that drove the early church. What kind of world did they envision? The New Testament clearly shows that the church was anticipating the glorious return of a judging Lord at an unknown date. It teaches that the world is not going to become a progressively lovelier place—quite the opposite, in fact (see Matt. 24:4-14; 2 Tim. 3:13; James 5:8; 1 Pet. 4:7). Evil and injustice are going to rage more ferociously as the final day draws closer.

And what kind of striving did this produce? As the following examples demonstrate, it led to a prioritization of witnessing, an emphasis on proclamation.

- At Pentecost, Peter says that he and his fellow apostles have been established as witnesses (proclaimers) of the exalted Christ whose enemies will soon be brought low, and calls on His hearers to save themselves from the generation that awaits such a fate (see Acts 2:32, 40).

- To the crowd that gathers in the temple after his healing a lame man, Peter says again that they are witnesses (proclaimers) to the resurrected Lord, who is awaiting the day when He will return and make all right (see 3:15, 19-21).

- In Cornelius' house, Peter declares that the first Christians were commanded to be witnesses (proclaimers) to the fact that Christ had been ordained judge of all (see Acts 10:39-42).

- Paul preaches (proclaims) in Athens that a day is coming when the world will be judged by the One God raised from the dead (see 17:30-31).

- Paul tells the Corinthians that a terrible vision of the Lord's coming in judgment causes us to engage in a ministry of persuasion (proclaiming)—pleading with men to be reconciled to God before it is eternally too late (see 2 Cor. 5:11, 18-20).

- And in Second Timothy 4, Paul exhorts Timothy to preach (proclaim) the gospel in light of the reality of Christ's return as judge, and because as that day approaches, men are less likely to listen (see 2 Tim. 4:1-5).

In passages like these, we see that the apostles have a clear vision of a world smoking and oozing like a rumbling volcano before the cataclysmic eruption of God's judgment. That sight, that knowledge of the world's fate, urgently compels them to be fanatic witnesses. Time is running out and there are many who don't know. This vision puts proclamation ministry in the driver's seat and all other kinds of ministries in the back of the bus.

These five reasons lead me to conclude that there is a real distinction in the New Testament Scriptures between an individual Christian's responsibility to show loving mercy to those around him or her and the corporate mission of the church to preach the gospel to all the world. As I said in the first part of the book, the Great Commission is paradigmatic. It alone explains what positive end we are working toward in the world. For all the good there is to be said about mercy ministry, it does not seem appropriate to designate it as the mission of the church toward the world.

Inspecting the Damage

I imagine that right about now you may be asking yourself, "What's the big deal? So what if some people are emphasizing mercy ministries? Is it really in competition with missions? Don't many people have a deep appreciation for both kinds of ministries?" These are the questions I want to talk about in this last section. It is my belief that an emphasis on deeds-based ministry will not exist in harmony with proclamation ministry. It will leech off of it, sapping its strength and hindering its growth. I will try to show why below.

Let's look at some of the thriving Western evangelical movements in recent years, especially those that have captivated many young people. More and more of these movements have insisted on the church's emphasis on things like cultural renewal, social justice, political activism and ministries of mercy. While some of these movements have also been characterized by a revival of preaching ministry, or even by awareness and concern for the world's unreached peoples, a dam remains between their movement and the world. Within these movements, it is a baffling, though far from uncommon, experience to talk to young people who have a love for the gospel and an appreciation for missions, yet who nevertheless have zero thought of being exported themselves! As a result, the movement's (or church's, or college's) exportation rate is abysmal. While I have no doubt that the leaders of such movements will doubt my diagnosis, I suggest that part of the problem in such movements is nothing other than their emphasis on mercy ministries. Why would this be?

The first reason I can think of is that an emphasis on deeds ministries redefines the need of the world in the minds of believers. As seen before, our perception of the need should and will affect our decisions. If we believe that the primary need in the world is to make disciples of Christ, then those places with a higher number of *unheards* turn a darker shade of red on our map. I must consider going to places like Bangladesh and Burkina Faso. But if I believe that there are two kinds of needs in the world for the church to address, ignorance of the gospel and temporal suffering, then the shape of our "need map" morphs considerably. Now there are new red places on your map—places that may already have a lot of gospel witnesses. Now when a missionary challenges you to go to a "very needy place," you point to the injustice and suffering around you and protest, "But there's so much to be done here!" I have found that many Western Christians sense the need of a particular place by counting social issues rather than counting *unheards*. They feel that staying where they are is justified because circumstances are quite bad for many people there. Indeed they are rightly sensitive to sin's multifarious effects in the world, yet they lack an ability to distinguish between kinds of needs.

The problem, as we saw earlier, is that the Bible doesn't exactly predict that mankind's condition will make an upswing before the end of the age. Suffering will continue to be a major part of the human experience on this earth. So if we decide that it is legitimate to stay in a given place just to meet material needs, it's unlikely we'll ever find a reason to move. Thus, when a church, college or movement begins to emphasize deeds-based ministry as an equally valid mission, it should not be surprising that many choose to remain in places that do not have a serious shortage of proclamation ministry. To them, the whole world is just one big needy place.

But this reason alone can't explain why, when faced with a decision between meeting these two kinds of needs, so many young believers should desire to work with deeds-based ministries over proclamation ministries. Here the second reason comes into play. Why does mercy ministry sap the strength of proclamation ministry? Because it is vastly easier! Now you won't find many mercy ministry advocates who will agree with that. They will truthfully explain to you the very real challenges of alleviating the suffering in this world. Then they say something like this, "This isn't as simple as just giving someone the gospel and then dusting off your hands and heading home." But this is a sad caricature of real proclamation ministry. I wonder if they would care to describe the apostle Paul's ministry of proclamation in those terms! He shows that there is a gritty, tortuous side to disciple making that is simply unparalleled in any kind of mercy ministry that I have ever encountered.

We regularly have mission trip groups visit us here in China, and we always try to put them to work doing Great Commission ministry, no matter how limited their time is. Many of them are surprised at the nature of the work we give them to do. They assumed that, coming to a nation less privileged than their own, there would be walls to paint, crops to harvest, wells to dig, orphans to feed, wounds to bandage or classes to teach. I have found, almost without exception, that to most of them the notion of trying to make disciples is far more intimidating than a day of hard manual labor. Give them a hospital full of handicapped children to feed and they'll plug away. Ask them to share their faith with unbelievers, and they have officially left their comfort zone!

What makes disciple making so much more arduous than other deeds? I'm sure there are a lot of factors at work. Many believers acutely feel their own insufficiency for teaching others how to follow Christ. Proclamation ministry involves speech, and to some there are no more terrifying actions than the movement of the mouth and the vocalization of air! There is the constant, paralyzing fear of rejection, which we rarely face when we are going about some charitable work for those in need.

Deeds ministry is also usually less personal than proclamation ministry. It is when confronting people with the truths of the gospel that we come to most fully understand who they are and the depths to which evil has taken root in their hearts. And certainly not least, there is a spiritual battle raging around us for the souls of men, which doubtless manifests itself in some of our deepest anxieties and misgivings. All of this means that if you tell Christians that there are two equally important missions in the church, you shouldn't be surprised if they all line up to meet "material needs."

A third reason why an emphasis on deeds-based ministry will hurt proclamation ministry is that it expends resources for the exportation of non-disciple-makers. When Western Christians do manage to turn their attention to the world, it is foremost the physical needs that we see in painful clarity. It is possible that such needs strike us so vividly because of the huge gap between our Western living standards and those that are common in other parts of the world. So when modern evangelical movements, colleges and churches get around to exporting some of their own resources, they often choose to send not those who are uniquely qualified to plant churches, proclaim the gospel and make disciples, but those who are qualified to teach English, practice medicine, repair engines and run small businesses. Thus, the resources that could be given to further the Great Commission are channeled toward those projects that are not oriented toward meeting the need for proclamation ministry.

In China, where I am privileged to work, this is excruciatingly evident. There is a huge number of "missionaries" on the ground here—far more than I would have expected when I came. But there are precious few disciple makers, so few proclaimers of the risen, returning Lord! Part of the reason this is so prevalent here is that China is technically a closed country (my friends in other restricted-access nations say that there is much of the same trend where they are). But it is now almost taken for granted among many believers that the "real need" that the Western church must meet in the developing world is not theological, evangelistic or ecclesiological, but material, physical and humanitarian. So more and more mission trips are taken to meet these "real needs." More and more laborers are sent forth to meet these "real needs." More and more organizations are established to tackle these "real needs." As a result, there are many places in the world that have a considerably high population of exported Western Christians, and the net gain in local proclamation ministry is practically nil!

Fourth, emphasis on deeds ministry impedes proclamation ministry because it hedges in those who do wish to preach the gospel. In other words, when we're told repeatedly that the greatest needs overseas are for Christian nurses and teachers, we begin to get the impression that there's not much for preachers to do there! Please don't mistake this for a remotely hypothetical problem! As discussed above, the Western church is experiencing something of a revival of interest in the ministry of proclamation. But this new crop of preachers is largely disinterested in missions, not because they're not interested in proclamation ministry, but because they're interested in proclamation ministry! They've been told that they can serve as preachers of the gospel in their own culture and in their own language. But those who go to labor as missionaries need to be prepared to repair generators, fly airplanes, harvest crops, pull teeth and pour foundations. After all, every mission trip they've ever taken was to roof a house or to feed orphans! Thus, while recent emphasis on proclamation ministry has magnified the glory of preaching the gospel to those without it, the simultaneous emphasis on deeds ministry has immobilized the preachers!

This is so common and so tragic. I regularly see young men who want to give themselves wholly to the work of church planting, disciple making and Bible teaching, but they seem unable to find a more needy place to do this work than a Midwestern town with a dozen other church plants! Though they find themselves stepping on the toes of other faithful pastors and church planters, it will not likely cross their minds to go to Thailand, where *unheards* abound. They have bought into the bizarre notion that those who stay preach, and those who go don't. The strong emphasis on deeds ministries so common in our churches effectively fences in those who would actually make the best missionaries!

A fifth reason that deeds-based ministry saps the strength of proclamation ministry is that in order to increase the value of meeting present-worldly needs, it is necessary to depreciate the value of meeting next-worldly needs. Meaning, if we portray lost souls and suffering bodies as equally important needs for churches to meet, does that not at least strongly imply that a lost soul is not a more serious condition than a suffering body? In the minds of many believers that I've met, such a conclusion seems only natural. Again, I'm in a huge Chinese city, where we are surrounded by all kinds of human suffering. If I campaign in the churches we've planted here for "holistic" ministry, it is tantamount to saying that a man's body and his soul are equally valuable. But a large part of our motivation for proclamation ministry is the surpassing value of an eternal soul in God's eyes. What does it profit a man if he gain his body—and the world with it—but lose his own soul? If God is only as interested in a soul as He is in a body, then expect believers to choose to minister to the body. That is, after all, the part of a man with which it is most natural for us to sympathize.

Many times I have heard preachers, in their passion for proclamation ministry, declare that the work of preaching the gospel does more to change men than the work of any politician, doctor, scientist or businessman. But many of those men, in their commitment to the cultural mandate and mercy ministry, will in other settings affirm that these other occupations are equally related to the church's mission in the world! Let's make up our minds, shall we? Either one of these labors is more valuable, or they're exactly the same. Is preaching the gospel really the most valuable, influential work in the world? Are souls really of so much more value than physical bodies that it'd be a wise trade to lose an eye or hand on the way to eternal life? It is very difficult to simultaneously maintain that these two kinds of ministries are equally valuable and that proclamation ministry is uniquely glorious! To elevate the one is to demote the other.

It would be a real challenge to find an organization that has consistently maintained the equality of these ministries over a long period of time! The deeds ministry side of their work will always edge proclamation out of the spotlight, and finally kick it headfirst off the stage. Movements that are today committed to worldwide disciple making had best beware before admitting mercy ministry as an equal; it has swallowed up many a movement in times gone by. In a three-legged race, the fastest runner can go no faster than the person to whom he's tied. Proclamation ministry suffers the same fate when bound to anything else. We should not wonder that the advance of the gospel seems so sluggish and the Word seems so restricted when we have taken steps to bind it to another ministry!

So for these sorts of reasons, proclamation ministry will not share the spotlight with deeds-based ministry. A strong emphasis on material needs and physical suffering undermines the ministry of the Word. If your church, school, organization or movement truly desires to export missionaries to the unreached millions worldwide, you are going to have to clearly explain to believers what is so uniquely important about proclamation ministry. You are going to have to choose to pour your resources into those endeavors that directly aim to give the gospel to more unbelievers.

A Concluding Hope

I am suggesting that believers and churches should think of their mission as proclaiming the gospel that saves men's souls and, whenever they can along that path, alleviating physical suffering (and doing a host of other things). Many believers are far more likely to think the reverse: that their ministry is alleviating physical suffering and, whenever they are able along that path, proclaiming the gospel. In other words, mercy ministry is controlling; proclamation ministry is squeezed in. This will continue until a clear emphasis is made on proclamation ministry over against all other kinds of ministries—until a clear line is drawn in the middle of the field and you stick up a sign on one side that says, "Welcome to Ohio."

Let's adjust our emphasis to proclamation ministry. Let us use our resources in the most important of ways: to increase the number of gospel presentations to unbelievers the world round. Let us make our decisions based on the Great Commission, reaching more and more *unheards*, while never failing to meet the needs of those whom we have opportunity to help along the way. If we fail to make this change, we will no doubt fail in our God-given mission, but we will also fail in the mission we substituted for it. The world is like the sinking Titanic. Do you want to pass out life jackets or try to improve the third-class passengers' living conditions?

Many Christians are enamored with the miracle-working aspects of Jesus' ministry and the great blessings it brought to the people of Israel for those few years. It is that kind of ministry that they most ardently hope to emulate. It has apparently never occurred to many of them that this is not the ministry of Jesus that they have benefited from personally! What the ministry of Jesus has meant for the world for almost two thousand years now has been the unique and unsurpassable work of atonement for sin. That is the ministry that brought me new life, that canceled my sin debt, that reconciled me to God, that made me His child, that declared me righteous, that is conforming me to the image of Christ, that seated me in heavenly places and that guaranteed my eternal life with God. That's the ministry that I want to join, and He has made a way for me to do just that! As I proclaim the Word to unbelievers in China, I am unlocking the door to incomparable glories. Little wonder that the Lord would say to His followers as they marveled at his miracles, "You will do greater works than these!" Sadly, many Christians seem committed to doing lesser works—works that aim for the same effects as Jesus' miracles, only with far fewer successes, far less power, far smaller spiritual significance and far more limited scope. Why not pick up the Word and do something greater?

11

Off Our Empires, Onto His Kingdom

How is the Commission at odds with our seeking of personal fulfillment?

Empire. What's the word bring to your mind? Caesar? Napoleon? British colonialism? Chinese dynasties? Mongol hordes? Darth Vader? All legitimate associations. What do all empires—even those in galaxies far, far away—have in common? Supreme authority of a single person or select group over a sprawling domain. Hence, even though they may lack the armies with cool explorer hats, we refer to businesses with massive reach and multitudinous operations as corporate empires. To build an empire is to bring more and more assets, realms, enterprises, populations and powers under one banner.

Is Not This Great Babylon?

The premise of this last chapter on changing emphasis is simple: every one of us has an imperial bent in our hearts. The same passion to conquer that created a Napoleon lies within you and me as well. We have an originally divine but now horribly deformed desire in our hearts to exercise authority over the world. Man truly was created by God in the beginning to have dominion over the earth, but then man packed his bags and tried to divorce himself from God. One of the things that he tried to take with him out of God's house was this desire for dominion. But, like everything else that he managed to fit into his suitcases for his journey into depravity, this desire never worked quite the way it had when it was at home with God (as we saw in chapter 8). Covetousness was born. The God-given ability to desire went haywire, with grasping desires flying wildly in all directions, clutching innumerable things that God never wanted us to have.

This is the engine of the imperialistic heart. Grasping at more and more, trying to bring all we see under the banner that bears our insignia. Let me cautiously attempt to show some of the ways that this wildcat empire building shows itself in our individual lives, in our churches and in miscellaneous Christian movements and organizations. It must be a cautious attempt because what I say here is based on forays into the dark ravines of my own heart. There I have found more than enough proof that I've got my own plots to conquer the world and build an empire for my own name.

What does it look like when people go about building their own empires? It shows first of all in an obsession with personal fulfillment. That is, as would-be emperors, we have a long wish-list outlining what we want our world and our lives to be like. In every one of our hearts, there are at least a few things that are strict nonnegotiables. They quite literally mean the world to us. Call them dreams, call them aspirations, call them life goals, but they all mean roughly the same thing: this is what my life is about, and I'm going to fight for it.

For some of us, these cravings are very ambitious and very specific. You have a very clear idea of what you want out of your life. You may have had it planned out perfectly since you were a kid. All your decisions have been made carefully to bring you to these goals. Maybe you were even praised by your parents and teachers as a focused go-getter. You are going to become an elected official. You are going to start your own business. You are going to make enough money so you can retire early and do whatever you want. You are going to found a charitable organization. You are going to attend an Ivy League school. You are going to be an artist. You are going to be a youth pastor. The things you want to accomplish in life are laid out clearly. You know just how you want your empire to expand.

Others of us have a more fuzzy set of desires. You may not be able to itemize your life goals systematically on a piece of paper, but you can nevertheless sense their presence in your heart. You want to live the good life: an interesting occupation, not harried with financial worries, regular time off to relax with friends, close proximity to extended family, fun-filled vacations and a comfortable home in which to raise your kids. Though this picture of the life you want is made more of sentiments than it is of any concrete measures, it is no less sure that you will do anything to realize it. Some emperors don't know which specific lands they want to conquer; they just know what kinds of lands they want!

"So what?" you say. "All this just shows that people have desires and goals. It doesn't make Napoleons out of us." But there's more to it than that. Empires aren't run by a board of directors. Whatever the emperor wants, the emperor gets—no matter what it takes. When we take our personal ambitions and set them up as the great ideals of our lives, we are acting just like a little emperor. In other words, there's nothing particularly self-important about aspiring to start a business. There is, however, something awfully presumptuous about making that the great, uncompromising ideal of your life, the thing that you've made a nonnegotiable for your existence. That's where we discover the imperial bent: we demand that all our resources be marshaled in order to achieve the growth of our domain. Our authority must grow. Our fame must grow. Our business must grow. Our ministry must grow. Our influence must grow. Our assets must grow. Our families must grow. Empire or bust.

We'll talk more about why personal empire building is such a presumptuous affront to God in a moment, but first I want to show that it's obviously not just individual believers who exhibit these imperialistic tendencies. Churches, colleges, organizations and Christian movements of every kind can all similarly idealize their own goals and agendas, and then set out to seek the growth of their ministry in those terms. This is certainly not to say that ministry growth is bad! There is cause to rejoice anytime that we see the growth of a gospel-preaching institution in this world! It is to say that making the growth of my ministry the loftiest and most vital aspiration of our lives is a goal with which any emperor could sympathize. Numbers are a great thing, and at times they show us real Great Commission progress. But when the numbers are important because they're *my* numbers, I have taken an imperial turn.

A Different Banner

It can be very bewildering for me to examine my own imperial aspirations because I have been taught, like many of my generation, that my desires are one of the primary ways that God communicates His will to me as a Christian. While it is true that the Holy Spirit works within us to produce desires to live for God, I don't know of anyone who thinks that all of a believer's desires are of this one kind! Most obviously, we all know that when we feel a strong desire to commit sin, this is not to be confused with the effects of the Spirit's operation! So we can't just rubber-stamp all the proposals that come across our heart's executive desk. Some of these desires have deep roots in our old, sinful nature! When we feel an inclination to do or pursue something, some hard analysis is required.

Lest you think I've now wandered completely off the map of this book's purpose, let me insert here that one of the greatest reservations young believers have about going into missions is that they don't desire such a life as much as they desire to work in business or live in America or some other thing. They see all their not-overtly-evil desires through theological lenses. They want to start a dance ministry because they think the Holy Spirit has given them that desire. They plan to become doctors because they feel they can't escape that passion! If that's you, let me first remind you of the highly suspect nature of your desires. Our sinful natures give both our desires and our thinking a naturally dictatorial slant (see Jer. 17:9; Eph. 4:17-22; James 4:1-3). You therefore should be suspicious of any desire that would obviously increase your power, wealth, fame, comfort, status or possessions. These are at least as likely to be the mindless gnawing of your zombie nature on your heart as they are to be the holy impulses of the Holy Spirit. It is our Christian duty to change the way we think and what we desire (see Rom. 12:2). Well, you think, what other kind of desires are there? If we suspect our desires for these kinds of good things, what's left to desire? Are we as Christians supposed to desire things that hurt us? Or are we to be unmotivated, passionless creatures with no plans or goals whatsoever? The answer to such questions is no, but we first need to see the banner of another kingdom before we can understand how this is possible.

Why is our empire building so offensive to God? Think of it this way: Why would it be offensive for Canada to march troops down to Bismarck and annex North Dakota for themselves? Because that territory already belongs to a sovereign nation! To claim it for themselves would be tantamount to an attack on the sovereignty of the United States. This is precisely what we need to realize about everything in this world that we may desire. Despite my self-deceiving imperial aspirations, every atom of this universe is the exclusive property of God, right down to my body and the air that I breathe (see Acts 17:25; 1 Tim. 6:17; James 1:17)! So when I decide to use my life (which is His) to pursue some things (which are His) that I want for myself, this is no less than a territorial infringement, an encroachment upon God's sovereign rule.

This righteous rule of God over that which He has created is referred to in the Bible as the "kingdom of God." It means that there is a banner under which every realm of this rebellious world is to be brought into subjection. All the kingdoms of the earth will ultimately become the kingdom of our God (see Isa. 9:7; Rev. 11:15). Now, as believers, we are presently living under that rule (see Mark 1:15; Luke 10:9-11; 11:20; Col. 1:13). As members of God's kingdom, we are to bring every part of our hearts into subjection to His rule and thus secure His claim over our lives (see Col. 1:9-14). Beyond this, we are given a mission from Christ to propagate the kingdom of God among others by the preaching of the gospel to secure His claim over the peoples of the world (see Acts 8:12; 28:23, 31). To live for our own desires is essentially to deny that we belong to a kingdom that has already claimed all for God!

The scene of our lives' work must be the kingdom of God, but to raise that banner, we must first take down our own. We have to scrap our own battle plans and quests for expansion before we can accept His marching orders (see Matt. 6:24). To pray that His kingdom would come is tantamount to praying that our empires would crumble (see 6:10)! How are we going to build this kingdom? Based on all that has been discussed in previous pages, I conclude that worldwide disciple making through proclamation of the gospel is the method whereby we as God's people can grow His kingdom on the earth. We call people to repent and trust in Christ because of the already present, yet impending nature of the kingdom of God (see 4:17). When people believe the gospel, they are transferred from the kingdom of darkness to the banners of God's kingdom (see Col. 1:13). Again we find that Christians cannot afford to make something other than the Great Commission the summary mission of their lives.

Does desire, then, not matter for the decision-making Christian? I believe it does. The better question is really which desires matter most. I think every true believer has, in addition to his heart's imperial desires, a sincere longing to see God's kingdom come. The problem is that our hearts seem to be unsure of the chain of command they are to follow. Is my empire more important, or does His kingdom take precedence? My point is not that Christians should not follow their desires, but rather that they should make the kingdom desire central and controlling, canceling out those longings that reek of the self-fulfilling old nature.

This means that, while I may have a desire to direct movies or decorate homes professionally, I need to make those desires subservient to the kingdom desire, the desire to expand the kingdom of God by making disciples worldwide. This desire may lead me back to my original plan of directing movies, but it may very well lead me to forsake that passion in favor of a work that will allow me to be more effective in proclaiming the gospel. I may find myself decorating a home at some point, but it is more likely that I will allow that dream to die in favor of a greater dream. What I want is only important as it lines up with what God wants, and He wants the world to hear. As true believers, that desire is unquenchably kindled like a glowing coal deep within us; we want the world to hear because God wants the world to hear. Making His kingdom my emphasis means that I will begin to make decisions that strip my empire of its titles, thrones, assets and authority, and then add fuel to my inward longing for God's kingdom to come.

There are some gifts and abilities that we glorify God with by *not* using them, sacrificing them to a surpassing desire! I have friends serving as missionaries all over the world who have left behind profitable businesses, scholarships, careers and even plentiful ministry opportunities at home. Some of their most exceptional and carefully-honed skills are gathering dust while they struggle to communicate the truths of the gospel in a foreign culture. To walk toward the world, they have walked away from wide open doors. They are not missionaries because they weren't good at anything else; nor did they analyze their gifts and decide they should serve overseas. It may surprise you, but, no, I had never dreamed of living in the frozen northeast corner of China. Rather, my brothers and I understood the mission and volunteered for service.

Are your life decisions being made for the kingdom? Have you chosen your path based on what you thought would do most to advance His kingdom's spread on the earth, or have there been other primary, driving factors? What are those nonnegotiable targets you're aiming to achieve? Have you set out to build your own glorious pyramids, your own monuments to self-fulfillment?

It's true: in order to go as an exported missionary to the world, you would have to let some monuments crumble. Some of your dreams would have to die. You would have to live your whole life without doing the things you always thought you would. I don't know a single missionary who couldn't think of something more personally fulfilling than carrying the gospel to places without it. There's not a lot of room for self-fulfillment in Zimbabwe; but there is room for kingdom-fulfillment there! If you would go there with the Word of Christ held high, ushering people from the domain of darkness to the kingdom of light, I think you would find that the glowing coal of passion within you could become a roaring inferno of desire and fulfillment!

What about your church? Are decisions being made with an emphasis on the worldwide progress of the gospel? That is no easy question to answer for most of us in positions of church leadership. As we've said, we feel like there's certainly some emphasis made on the kingdom's growth—and that's worth rejoicing over. But how do we tell if some of the church's decisions are still buried in imperialism? How can we decide if we're more committed to achieving our own fulfillment than to the advance of the gospel worldwide? Below are just a few thoughts about the difference between empire growth and kingdom growth. Notice how each characteristic of empire growth runs against the grain of the Great Commission. To emphasize our own empires is to grind the gears of the church's mission backwards!

Empire Growth Envisions Height, Kingdom Growth Envisions Breadth

Like our ancestors who built at Babel, there is little that comes as naturally to us as trying to reach for the stars. We want to climb to great heights—our skyscraping aspirations demand that we accumulate more and more, standing atop a growing mountain of hoarded resources. Emperors demand tribute, and they never like to see resources, be they dollars or ministry leaders or church members, walking out the door.

This is unfortunate, because that is exactly what obedience to the Great Commission requires. To fulfill our mission, it is necessary for us to push out with every resource at our disposal! If we put an emphasis on worldwide disciple making, we will lose valuable members of our churches and our staffs. Our sons and our daughters will volunteer to go to dangerous places. Scary amounts of money will begin to drain from our budgets. Why? Because the Great Commission is all about breadth, about spreading the gospel to all corners of the earth. For such an end, Christ expended His all. He was emptied! Crushed! Pressed down so that life would flow to the nations! How could we think that we could seek His kingdom by accumulating rather than disseminating?

Let me give you one example of the way that height and breadth are often swapped as biblical visions for our churches. It is more and more common to hear about the importance of our churches working to change their surrounding society and culture. For all the talk currently in vogue about transforming culture, there is no vision in the Bible of so-called "Christian cultures" or "Christian nations" or, you might say, places where the church's resources are so concentrated in one place that they pervade the surrounding society. That is a vision of height. A vision of so much Christian influence in one place that even unbelievers are benefited. On the contrary, when the Bible paints the picture of the end the church is working towards, it talks about Jesus' worldwide name recognition (breadth), not the moral reformation of sinners alienated from him! Of course, I realize that there are benefits that unbelievers receive from living in proximity to believers; but such benefits are incidental by-products of the church's real mission: the worldwide broadcasting of the gospel.

Here's another example. It's easy to talk about our churches being committed to the worldwide spread of the gospel, yet it is equally easy to overlook how extreme such a commitment can be. There is very little consideration in most churches, for example, of sending the pastoral leadership away as missionaries. The modern mentality says, "If you can get a Paul or a Barnabas to join your staff, pay them whatever it takes to get them to stay!" Most pastors certainly aren't considering going themselves! Why? If the breadth of the gospel is our primary concern, shouldn't we see the top layer of church leadership in the most-reached places spilling over into the least-reached places, like water splashing over the top of a dam? So why is that so rare to see? Because that would be an unacceptable blow to the empires that many churches and preachers have been building!

Speaking of Paul, was there ever a person so committed to the breadth of the gospel's advance, even at the expense of the height of his own ministry? Think just of the periods Paul spent incarcerated. Quite beyond the physical discomfort of a prison cell, the average highly-motivated pastor has reason to shudder at Paul's circumstances. What would happen to our ministries? Most of us fear what will happen to our churches if we miss a single Sunday! Imagine the nightmares of an indefinite jail sentence, completely unable to protect your life's work! But Paul, stuck in a Roman prison, still finds joyful thanksgiving in abundant supply (see Phil. 1:18-21; 4:4-13)! Paul smiles in his cell, knowing what his bonds have accomplished! He sees the ways that the gospel is being advanced through his persecution. His guards have heard the gospel. His friends have been embold-ened. Those who dislike him have even tried to hurt him in some way by preaching the gospel—a plan that could have used some more time on the drawing board (see Phil. 1:12-18)! Loss of comfort, freedom, reputation and influence all seem to leave a surprisingly small dent in Paul's happiness! In spite of the fact that his personal ministry was being suppressed, Paul rejoiced to know that the borders of the gospel were expanding. Though the influence of the Apostle Paul Evangelistic Ministries, Inc. was at an all-time low, the spread of the gospel was at an all-time high. And Paul rejoiced.

What if the greatest contribution we could make for the ad-vancement of the gospel were to cost us the height of our influ-ence, reputation, status and comfort? It is certainly true that all of those things are potential tools for the progress of our mis-sion. It is also true that many men are clinging to paltry scraps of influence and status, insisting that such "talents" somehow pre-clude them from becoming unknown and unsung as missionar-ies to lowly fields. We point to the good we are doing where we are, as a pass to not consider the good we could do elsewhere. Paul gave up far more to see the gospel seep into new territories. If we hope to see the gospel penetrate further in our day, it will require many believers—and many of their pastors—to lay their own name, their current ministry and their financial security on the altar of kingdom breadth.

Empire Growth Focuses on Today, Kingdom Growth Focuses on the Future

I sincerely love, and am thankful for, the missionary who has been a mentor to me for almost a decade, but sometimes I want to strangle him (I'm sure the feeling is mutual!). The last time I was back in the States, we had just passed the four-year threshold of our time in China. We had a long meeting at his house to discuss the progress of the ministry so far and some plans for the next couple years. I was kind of hoping for a big pat on the back, I think. Instead he sobered me, as mentors must often do, with the disquieting fact that my career as a missionary in China was probably—statistically, anyway—20 percent over, or something along those lines. More, if I get myself booted out of the country! He drew my attention away from past accomplishments and directed it toward the frightfully large task that still remains in China. Typical of him, really. He has been relentlessly future-focused since I met him.

This has been tremendously helpful to me as a missionary. During the writing process for this book, my family and I were deported from China. On Easter Sunday, teams of police descended onto the worship services of the churches we had planted in the city. After long hours of questioning from the police, we were given ten days to get out of the country. They say we will not be allowed to enter again for five years. The following ten days were the most difficult of my life. The pain of being torn away from my Chinese brothers and sisters, many of whom are more like sons and daughters to me, still lingers. Beyond that, my work in mainland China, the work that thrilled me so much and that I had poured myself into with abandon, was suddenly ended. It turned out that the twenty percent that my missionary mentor had cautioned me about was really more like seventy percent! But I am so thankful for his prodding back then. Thankfully, the churches, pastors and believers have continued, not without some bumps, to serve Christ.

Now many of the supports are removed and we are discovering what will stand and what will fall when I am removed from the equation. This is a question that is usually easy to ignore just as long as everything stands today, when my name is connected to it! If churches close, men fall away and the gospel witness shrivels when I am gone, it's unlikely many will blame me. I will probably be able to get over it eventually (I understand that death helps ease some of those anxieties!). But if my concern is God's kingdom and not my own empire, then the stability of the work after my presence is removed is of key importance. The kingdom calls us to be future-focused.

It's not just church planters in closed countries who need to learn to number their days. All Christians committed to the mission must live with a fervent sense of urgency. The Great Commission does not allow us to fritter away our days, weeks, months and years without reflecting on our effectiveness in disciple making. We have been given a gigantic goal, and our own mortality has given us a limited time in which to work for that goal. Accordingly, we find that God's Word tells us in several places to value the time given to us and to make the best use of it. There is a countdown on the board. The Christian's time is far more valuable than the final seconds of the fourth quarter in the Super Bowl! As long as there is Great Commission work to be done, there is no place for believers to feel satisfied with their past accomplishments. As long as there is more time left on the clock, we must, as my mentor says, "work like wild men" for the kingdom!

Regrettably, there are many modern believers who seem to have confused the peace of God with laziness, apathy and aimlessness. They have attained a sort of Christian nirvana, where nothing moves them and they move nothing! These spiritual sloths are totally unconcerned with how long it takes to obey the

Father's commands and are totally blind to the consequences of this sluggishness. Though some of these may imagine that their impassivity is a result of their theological orthodoxy (e.g. their trust in the sovereignty of God), the ambitious hustle of kingdom laborers throughout history betrays their error. Their view of God is clearly of a different sort than the one that drove the apostle Paul, who liked to compare his ministry to a race. You might blame your sloth on Calvinism, but you'd be hard-pressed to blame it on Calvin!

So if it's not necessarily theological, why are so many modern believers wallowing in inaction, and not working for the kingdom's growth? Because the slothful man already has his empire! His domain may not look like much to those on the outside, but to this emperor, it's all he really needs to be happy. He's got his bass boat, his widescreen, his golf buddies, his son's football team, his new building, his leisure time, his library or his pulpit! Thus, the siren of the Great Commission is not enough to awaken the emperor from his contented slumber. He's got what he wants, and he couldn't be bothered with the mission.

How great a danger this poses to believers living in modern first world nations, in the midst of an endless craze for creature comforts! A constant stream of new desserts, mattresses, gadgets, fashions, television dramas, sports seasons and spa therapies all serve to deaden our resolve and cushion our thrones. It is hard to live in an Acts-like state of mind when life is so . . . well, comfortable! Everything in our affluent society works together to lull us into a sense of complacency; and our enemy happily exploits this condition to keep us from awakening to our grave responsibility!

One place where I am always disturbed to discover this sluggishness is on the campuses of Bible colleges and seminaries. Many students exhibit little concern over how many years they will spend before finally launching into Great Commission work. Now, I would not diminish the value of education by one iota, but it is tragic to see so few students in a hurry to get out into the harvest fields! That easygoing, latte-sipping, carefree attitude so typical of student life is totally at odds with the urgency of the church's mission. I would be the last to suggest a missionary go underprepared, but I don't often find students meandering through many years of college because they believe it to be necessary training for kingdom impact! Instead, their college years are marked by indecision and diversion. More than most, Christian twenty-somethings need to wake up to the reality that as they squander their days, God's command goes unobeyed, and souls lie in the darkness outside of God's kingdom. They need to look up at the seconds ticking down on the scoreboard.

Empire Growth Fosters Dependency, Kingdom Growth Fosters Maturity

At the hub of many churches and ministries both at home and on mission fields stands a single, irreplaceable person who holds everything together. Or maybe a small core of irreplaceable people. Nothing can really get done in the church unless the pastor (or some other significant leader) is integrally involved. No one else can preach, no one else can organize, no one else can write, no one else can take responsibility.

While this may seem like an unfortunate role into which some pastors of smaller churches find themselves roped, it is not uncommon to find that growing, thriving churches and ministries are still largely a one-man show. In these situations, there is usually no shortage of volunteers to lend a hand, so why is the focus staying on one person?

As the majority of my observations and experiences have been limited to the foreign field, let me lay out for you how this works in a missionary's ministry. The missionary starts a church in a foreign culture. No one knows how to do anything except for him. After some time, though, the church begins to grow. Maybe more churches are started. Yet the missionary continues to do everything himself. He preaches in all the churches. He keeps them all afloat financially. He leads all the evangelistic outreach. He teaches all the seminary courses. There is a conspicuous lack of local leadership everywhere he goes!

Ask him why, and you'll likely get an earful about the sad state of education and parenting in the country. He'll explain that the local culture all but guarantees that young men will be ill-suited for ministry. People just won't serve faithfully in the church. Rarely do you get the real answer: no one does it as well as I do, and I'd rather not take the time to teach them!

I fear this dynamic is strong in American churches as well. There seems to be a growing willingness to put an enormous weight of resources behind one personality in a church or ministry. To give an example, the Western vision of a successful church looks increasingly like one man preaching via satellite to a host of different locations. While there is great cause to rejoice over the thousands sitting under the preaching of the gospel, the reason given for this particular strategy of expansion is worrisome. We are usually told, "This leader is uniquely gifted at communicating. So we're going to get other people to do everything else, and we'll let him handle the preaching." All other considerations of such a strategy aside, are we really to believe that this person is a more effective communicator than anyone else could learn to be with the right training? Though it may be argued that such a threat may be avoided, it must be admitted that there is an enormous danger of building a huge church that is largely dependent on one man. The future stability of these churches is precarious, to say the least.

Of course, very few churches achieve this ideal. But many smaller ministries exhibit just as much dependency as larger personality-driven organizations. In such ministries, the vision, service and resources are all centered on one individual. This is dependency, and it's the stuff of which empires are made! What exactly is it in my heart that enjoys being needed in Chinese churches? Why do I feel an urge to laugh maniacally when I discover that more and more people are coming under my direction and authority? Because I've got imperial blood.

One other related effect of the imperial desire is that it serves to undercut teamwork and cooperation among believers. Personally, I am not of the number that believes that all the missions organizations in the world should be rolled together into one giant, ecumenical entity. I do believe, though, that we ought to demonstrate the same willingness to rejoice in the Great Commission work of other believers that we see in the ministry of Paul. There is simply an enormous amount of overlap in the outreach efforts of churches in many of the world's more evangelized regions. If kingdom growth was our primary focus, we might be able to conclude, "There are many of us preaching the gospel here, so let me leave this region to others and move on to another, less evangelized place." But as empire growth is our focus, it seems the work of others doesn't count! It doesn't matter how many other churches could take up the slack, emperors feel they must stay behind and tend to this region personally.

Now, think about how contrary all of this is to the mission. When it commands us to make disciples, the Great Commission presupposes that we will be able to train others effectively. That we will be producing leaders just as mature as ourselves, who will even be able to teach subsequent generations! We are not to be the only people on the team who can score! If we look around and see that our church has one supporting pillar, this is a sure sign that we will not effectively grow the kingdom worldwide. If the churches we've planted in China are forever dependent upon us, it will be because we have failed in our Great Commission duty, and our kingdom influence will be small. To work for the kingdom's expansion requires that we build men and churches that will not be dependent upon us, but will be mature enough to become independent gospel-proclaiming agents.

The End of All Empires

In each of these chapters about emphasis change, we have examined key factors that must figure into how believers and churches make decisions about allocating the resources God has entrusted to us. These are a few of the ways that we can ensure that we are putting an emphasis on the mission that God has left for us. Of our time, manpower, finances, planning and prayers, how much is being used to make disciples out of *unheards*?

We have talked about not just a theological problem or a strategic question, but a deep spiritual issue. Are we willing to abandon our plans and our goals when they are found to be at cross purposes with God's stated mission for his church? When the advance of God's kingdom infringes upon our empire's borders, what will our reaction be? Let me reiterate one last time that I haven't been speaking about the overtly sinful desires of our hearts. Even good and noble ambitions and aspirations must be rooted out when they stand in the way of God's kingdom.

At this juncture, John the Baptist's attitude is worth internalizing. When he is approached about the departure of many of his disciples to sit under Jesus' ministry, he responds that Christ must increase and he must decrease. This whole chapter has been about that increasing and decreasing. Notice that John says "must!" As John sees the candle of his influence flicker and begin to wane, what is it that gives him peace? How does he not lose his head and start a bitter campaign to call back all that he's lost? It is the knowledge that, though an emperor may work his whole life to amass and accumulate assets, it must decrease. It will not remain! Eventually every emperor meets his end. Your cyborg apprentice turns on you suddenly (in the middle of your lightning attack on his estranged son) and chucks you one-handed into a pit. Or you get exiled to a tiny island. Or you might enjoy an entirely more pedestrian though no less conclusive end. Your mark on the world will largely wash away like so many footprints on a beach.

For John, attached to that certainty is the knowledge that the kingdom of Christ must increase. This also is inevitable. When we have used our resources to exalt Christ, this becomes the greatest news we could receive. The kingdoms of this world must become the kingdom of our God, and He must reign forever and ever! Our labors for our own empires will prove to be of little worth, for the sun will finally set on our monuments, and our palaces will become rubble. But our labors for His kingdom will prove to be far more valuable than they ever appeared, when the dawn of Christ's rule at last gives way to the day of his eternal glory. In that day, we will rejoice to have had a meaningful part in his kingdom's establishment! When we gaze unblinking toward that glowing horizon, we will joyfully rush to employ all of our investments, all of our assets, all of our claims and all of our days to pave the way, like John before us!

12

In the Huddle

What steps can be taken to meaningfully contribute to the mission?

One of my most ambitious goals for this book has been that it would serve as a sort of pep talk for Christians, urging them to cast themselves without reservation into the Great Commission. I'm not sure if I have accomplished this, but I am comforted knowing that there are far more eloquent, inspiring voices in the church calling believers to disciple-making action. There are many faithful men and women stirring up godly passion for the unreached among evangelical churches. In fact, I would venture a guess that the majority of people who read this book are those who are already fired up about the Great Commission.

Pep Talks and Playbooks

But when we talk about the Great Commission, "pep" isn't the only kind of talk that needs to be given. As you have surely experienced, pep talks do not always have the desired result. A coach may charge up his peewee team with some inspiring words about winning, only to watch them run the football the wrong way down the field in the next play! Emotional fervor does little good if there isn't a clear plan for channeling that energy into positive yardage. Pep talks must always be supplemented with "direction talks." This has been my primary hope for those readers who are already convinced of the paradigmatic importance of worldwide disciple making: that we would together consider upon what trajectory this commitment to missions should set our lives.

Though many of the Great Commission's ramifications for our lives can be found sprinkled throughout the discussions in this book, I would like to take an entire chapter to speak plainly about how a commitment to worldwide disciple making might change your life. This seems necessary, because I for one never cease to be mystified by the directions believers run after they are infused with missions' zeal! Possibly because foreign missions seems far removed from our normal, domesticated lives, it seems to be the theater of boundless creativity! Part of being a veteran missionary involves serving as an audience for all sorts of sales pitches for new missions ideas. I've heard passionate presentations for missionary plans involving horses, baseball, dancing, dojos, murals, coffee and solar panels. None of these are bizarre caricatures of missionary strategies, but only a sampling of the innovation so common among Christians who are passionate about the Great Commission! There's just no telling what a person zealous for world missions will run off and do!

A missionary can only rejoice to discover Christian brothers and sisters' commitment to God's glory and compassion for the lost, yet in the end he often walks away frustrated by their ill-advised plans for involvement! Over and over, I have listened to students explain to me their plan to go to China to teach English, to go to the Middle East to work in a coffee shop, to backpack around the world for a year, to switch their major to international business or to train to get their pilot's license. It's a bit like watching ripe fruit fall from the tree and split open on rocks below. Zeal for missions they have; direction in missions they have not.

And so, the church's "Great Commission playbook" seems to get thicker and thicker as the years go by. Though it would take another, much longer book (not to mention a much more qualified author) to discuss the merits and drawbacks of all these multitudinous strategies, I would like to use this chapter to offer a few suggestions about how to begin wisely directing your zeal for missions. What should your next play look like? In which direction should your respective "X" or "O" run to be of maximum impact in obeying the Great Commission? Before we answer that question, let's first observe what goes hopelessly wrong with so many well-intentioned endeavors to serve in missions.

Where Plays Break Down

Feathers may be ruffled already. In talking about China, for instance, people get very defensive about the English teaching strategy. I couldn't begin to count the times someone has explained to me that Christian English teachers can get away with talking about the meaning of Easter or Christmas in Chinese schools, like it was the cleverest scheme ever hatched. It's hard to make them see that, as we're planting churches and preaching the gospel openly in China, such a plan isn't terribly appealing to our team! Why don't you ask your pastor in America why he doesn't get a job teaching in a local middle school and slyly slip subliminal gospel messages into his lessons every Christmas and Easter? This is a prime example of a largely misdirected missions strategy that nevertheless has huge appeal to missions-loving believers. Though you may disagree with my judgment about this particular play, what in general is it that makes any missions strategy unbefitting our playbook?

First, many missions plans fail because they are not direct enough. That is, they add steps into the process of obeying the Great Commission. These steps might be called pre-Commission efforts. In the example about teaching English in China, missions-minded believers want to go to China, preach the gospel and make disciples. Teaching English is obviously none of those things, but these Christians have been told that a teaching job is a necessary prerequisite to doing what they really want to do. So they make an educational career the foundation of their plan for bringing the gospel to China and, in so doing, insert a gap between themselves and the actual Commission work that motivated them to go to China in the first place!

The same could be said for many other plays. Promising to "open doors," they actually pass over countless obvious opportunities to make disciples. Help some farmers harvest their crops and hope for a chance to share the gospel. Walk around a park and hope for a chance to share the gospel. As I understand, in a football game it's never a good idea for a rushing player to run the ball backwards for a chance to run around defenders the long way! More often than not, it will result in lost yardage. You will run backwards far longer than you planned, if your opponent has anything to do with it! Such missionary strategies might make interesting Rube Goldberg machines, but they are not a wise way to carry out the Great Commission.

These pre-Commission plans are especially predominant in countries where there are significant risks attached to preaching the gospel. Taking time here to discuss a biblical perspective on persecution would carry us past the borders of this book's concern. Let me simply say in this regard that the desire to avoid persecution is a poor basis for missionary play-calling. It will rarely lead to the kind of decisions we see the apostles making in the book of Acts. Thus, a plan to avoid persecution at all costs will result in precious little in the way of Great Commission progress. It will shy away from every opportunity to make disciples that might pose a potential threat to one's personal safety.

As we'll discuss in a moment, the most direct thing you could do to be involved in missions is to personally begin to prepare to go as a missionary yourself! To go on an extreme mission trip with the express purpose of ascertaining your own usefulness in a different place. To actually sell your house and car, raise some financial support, get some training, and go as a gospel-preaching disciple maker to a very unreached corner of this world. Strangely, this seems to be the one thing that the creativity of impassioned believers cannot dream up! If you have a heart filled with zeal for missions, I beg you to consider first whether or not it would be wise for you to go all in and become an exported missionary yourself. Only after that possibility has been cleared off the table should you consider some other, more indirect means of involvement in the Great Commission.

Another reason that missions plays break down is that they are not radical enough. The mission left to us by Christ describes an emergency of epic proportions. Billions have not heard of what Christ achieved on the cross! Drastic measures are called for. When the clock is running down and his team is still far from the end zone, the coach will flip to the "extreme" part of the playbook! Unfortunately, many of the plays discussed in our church's huddles are just too lackadaisical and workaday to be of much use in the field as it currently lies! There is no place for halfhearted tipping of our hats to the needs of the world—occasionally remembering the nations in prayer when we happen to think of it, supporting missionaries who happen to cross our paths and encouraging those in our congregations who happen to feel called to be missionaries. Here are a few examples.

Take, for instance, our financial involvement in the work of missions. Most believers would agree that we should each personally be giving to support the advance of the gospel worldwide. And we'd agree that our churches ought to allocate a portion of their budget to do the same. The question becomes, then, how much is enough? Potential to make progress in missions is often lost because we fail to answer that question radically enough!

I'll never forget a small pastors' conference I attended in rural North Carolina several years ago. The conference's emphasis was on the pastor's role in world evangelization, and a pastor from a tiny, remote town up in the mountains was scheduled to preach during one of the sessions. Later I would learn that this pastor's small church was committed financially to missions in a measure out of all proportion to its size. Leading that charge of radical missions giving was this pastor himself, who still worked a job outside the church to pay his own bills. I remember him saying in his afternoon message, "I hear many pastors telling their congregations that if they give up a bag of potato chips every day they can help support missionaries around the world. Let me tell you something: God's not after your potato chips!" What did he mean? Simply that, when faced with the emergency of the lost world, if we are still thinking in terms of our daily snacks, we are not being radical enough!

Then there are also ways in which those who do export themselves fail to be sufficiently radical. For example, some of them have set their hearts on being exported to places that are still characterized by a fairly low unreached factor! There are a large number of churches and a relatively small number of people who have never heard the gospel before. While these missionaries' willingness to move themselves is praiseworthy, it will result in little Great Commission progress if they do not go to a place where there are a significantly larger number of *unheards*. The decision to do so will certainly be difficult, for those fields with higher unreached factors are generally much more difficult for missionaries to live and minister in.

It's also possible to not be radical enough in our pacing. In the last chapter, it was mentioned that many students are not completing their education with a sense of urgency. Often even those who are confident that they are eventually going to work in foreign missions have no plans to arrive at a foreign field before they're in their midthirties. That may sound plenty young to you. But try to learn a difficult language when you're past thirty! Try to raise support and move to another country when you have a few kids. (Not to mention the difficulties of prying them from their grandparents' grip!) Try to adjust to the challenges of adapting to a new culture and planting a new ministry from scratch. Those are just a few of the reasons that you might want to set a more radical pace—one that will get you to the field with an extra decade or so to work!

Again, about the most radical play you could make personally would be to go as a missionary yourself! What more drastic step could you take than to move your family to the heart of a population of *unheards*, learn to speak their language and proclaim the gospel to them in churches that you plant? Before you rule out such a measure for its impracticability and the fallout likely to ensue, remember that the gospel itself is a story about drastic steps—drastic steps taken by the most holy God to redeem sinful man! It is the news, so good and blessed and powerful to those who believe, that God took direct, radical action in the work of salvation.

Whatever your plans for involvement in the Great Commission, take a second to consider how direct and how radical the play you're calling is. Are there some steps you could take that would more directly engage the world's unreached people with the gospel message? If so, what are your reasons for choosing such an indirect route? Are there more radical measures you could take—measures that would testify to the mission's urgency and gravity? If so, what exactly holds you back from a more extreme level of involvement?

Why Not?

In the remaining pages of this chapter, I want to address directly some of the different entities that the Great Commission concerns. Again, this is a "direction talk" more than a pep talk. As I said above, these are just some suggestions. These are admittedly some of the most hard-hitting, most radical plays that we could possibly run. I hope all of us in this huddle will together agree that these are just the kind of things that will result in significant forward movement of the gospel around the world.

I phrase each suggestion as a "why not" question. The reason is that each of these suggestions is based upon the task that the group in question would seem to be most uniquely qualified to perform. These questions aim to reinforce the utter reasonableness of getting involved at this radical of a level. Just like a football coach might say to a prospective player at tryouts, "You throw the ball very well. You have a great eye for the action on the field and you make great decisions under pressure. Why not try playing quarterback?" The call of the Great Commission requires that there be believers doing all of the tasks suggested below. I hope you will look at your qualifications and ask, "Why not me?"

A Play for Young People—Why Not Go?

The current condition of the world requires that many believers go as exported disciple makers. In any church, there is no demographic more suitable for the task of leaving one's own cultural context to preach the gospel to millions of *unheards* than believers in their twenties. This thought has already been somewhat developed in previous chapters, so I won't beleaguer the point. Let me quickly review some of the factors that should lead twentysomethings to strongly consider running the route assigned to this particular "X" in the playbook.

The most difficult languages (like Arabic, Hindi, Cantonese, etc.) will take a few years for even the most fertile of minds to learn at an effective level. The challenges of adapting to a culture vastly different than one's own are best taken into stride by those who are in a transitional period of life anyway. The younger children are when they arrive on the mission field, the better their chances of making a smooth transition to the target society. There are many inevitable pitfalls lying ahead in the missionary's path. The longer the time he has to extricate himself and learn from his own experience, the more effective he will prove to be. As can be seen in ministry in general, there are some wonderful benefits that are reaped simply due to a lengthy tenure of service in a single ministry position. None of these factors eliminate the possibility of there being wisdom in exporting an older believer; they only maximize the possibility of a younger one being exported!

My wife and I moved to China and began full-time language training when we were both twenty-three years old. At the time, we had been married three months (which was the minimum amount of time my mentor would allow). Though those months at the beginning of our lives together and our ministry in China were plagued with one stressful event after another, we were still just happy newlyweds! Most of the team of missionaries with whom I work began their careers at a similarly young age. So I have repeatedly seen firsthand the extremely positive effects of going to the mission field as a young couple as well as the comparative challenges of going at an older age (older here meaning over thirty).

So why not go? Whether you are single or just starting off your married life, please see for a moment the potential glory that could result from you giving the rest of your life to the mission! Asking an older saint to do so would be asking much less! But a young believer laying down their remaining decades as a worshipful sacrifice to the Lord speaks far more highly of the immeasurable worth of the cause and its Master. There is certainly no more direct or radical way that you can be obedient to His command. There are millions of *unheards* in Tunisia, Kyrgyzstan and Thailand—why not personally go directly to them and give them the gospel? Do you think you'd regret it? Do you think they'd regret it?

A Play for Churches—Why Not Send?

Perhaps due to the multiplication of parachurch missionary organizations, the church's role in worldwide disciple making has become increasingly indirect. For some missionaries, announcing their plans to go to another country has the same practical effect as announcing a plan to switch membership to another church. That is, the relationship is essentially over! Maybe the missionary family will come back for a visit when they're home from the field, but the church at large has either no desire or no knowledge of how to be positively, meaningfully involved in the lives of their members who are exported to a foreign field. Thus, many missionaries feel divorced from their church, as if they have walked unnoticed out the back door.

About the highest expectation that some have for churches' missions involvement is financial. Western churches in particular are often told that the greatest contribution they could make to the missionary effort worldwide is to give of the money with which they have been disproportionately blessed. Sometimes the church is entrusted with a bit more responsibility: prayer. They can pray for more laborers to enter the harvest fields, and they can pray for those who have already gone out. Certainly no less can be asked of our churches. But are there any more direct, more radical ways that churches can be involved in the Great Commission work?

What if a church resolved to proactively seek to export disciple makers into fields around the world? To use every resource at their disposal to press upon their members' hearts the demands of the mission. To maintain a volunteer spirit, encouraging every member, starting with the staff, to make themselves available for the missionary enterprise, should the congregation deem them fit. To train, guide, support, visit and encourage those sent out from their midst to the nations. In my lifetime, I have been privileged to see a few congregations of this rare breed. They are wartime churches—churches that exist to raise armies for the worldwide battle we have been dispatched to fight.

Have you ever heard someone say, usually to Sunday school teachers or other workers who deal with ministry to children, "You never know who you're teaching! One of those little brats in your class may turn out to be a great pastor or missionary someday!" In the wartime kind of churches I'm talking about, they have a slightly different attitude. They're not wondering if some child may end up becoming a missionary; instead, they're working intentionally and diligently to make missionaries out of all the kiddos! They're more surprised when a young person doesn't want to be an exported disciple maker than when one does!

So why not send? Why not organize everything your church does around the mission? You won't get everyone to go, but what if 10 or 15 percent of your congregation did? Would that not be one of the most radical, game-changing plays that your church could make?

A Play for Missions Organizations—Why Not Strategize?

For better or for worse, missions organizations currently shoulder a lot of the responsibility for mobilizing the church's resources toward the Great Commission. As was just mentioned, when a missionary goes out, his relationship with his sending church often fades into the background. In many cases, the only entity that even attempts to be a replacement family of fellowship and accountability for the missionary is his missions organization. Their role has typically been to undertake projects and serve missionaries in ways that would likely be impossible for the average local church. So, as the networking structure linking missionaries to each other and to churches back home, missions organizations unquestionably have been designated as the primary strategists for advancing the gospel worldwide.

It seems hard, however, to justify the massive amount of overhead created by the huge and growing number of evangelical missions organizations. Each office, secretary, training facility and director represents a significant drain on the flow of resources to the mission field. The burden of proof, then, lies with the missions organizations to demonstrate that these investments by the church have not been in vain. I personally believe that such a demonstration is certainly possible.

If you genuinely believe that the best play you can make for Great Commission impact is to become yet another appendage to the structures of a missions organization, why not work to make your agency intensely strategic? I know that there are wonderful exceptions, but these organizations have a tendency (common to organizations of every kind) to drift towards bureaucracy, complexity and mediocrity. And while nonprofits and relief agencies may be able to live with less than optimal performance, our mission is not so trifling as to allow such passivity. If a missions organization charged with the investment of so many resources does not have a clear and radical strategy for making a specific impact on the lost world, it would be better for them to close up shop and leave the task to others. Of course, as an organization mired in bureaucracy is never likely to vote for its own liquidation, my suggestion would naturally be for those who support it from without to cease doing so.

So what kind of strategy should a missions organization have? Again, this is a question that deserves a long and nuanced answer. Since this is just a place for suggestions, I would only repeat that direct and radical action is needed. The requirements to be a missionary with your agency perhaps need to be intensified. The geographic region that your agency is focused on may need to be narrowed. A watchful eye must be kept on the agency's budget.

But the place where missions organizations need to spend the most time carefully strategizing is in their role of choosing where missionaries will be dispatched. Not every agency exercises a high degree of control over where missionaries go, but even those agencies without such authority should not underestimate the influence they can have in a missionary's decision making. Enough has been said in previous chapters about the kinds of places to which the Great Commission sends us that we need not repeat it here, but such questions should be foundational to a missions organization's existence. Are missionaries with your agency going to urban areas? Are they working in places with high *unheard* factors? Are they learning to preach the gospel in the local language? Are they planting churches?

In too many organizations, the "where" questions are now just being answered in terms of people groups. Some of the missions organizations with greater control over their missionaries' field choices have sought to reposition them based on the information fed to them by researchers mapping out unreached tribes and other ethnolinguistic groupings. The difference between a traditional model of the mission and a people-groups model is not a small one: the people-groups model continues to lead missionaries away from cities, away from church planting, and away from millions who have yet to hear the gospel (who happen to belong to 'reached' peoples). For what it's worth, I would plead with all such agencies to consider carefully whether or not their plans are based on little more than a faddish interpretation of the Great Commission.

A Play for Givers—Why Not Partner?

For a book on missions, not a lot has been said so far about giving. Without a doubt, the financial support of missionaries and their ministries is a key part of any play that we decide to run. The New Testament speaks enough about this subject to give us certainty that the opportunity to be financially involved with a missionary project is a graciously God-given one, and one that we should steward zealously (see, for example, Phil. 4:10-19). But, as with all kinds of zeal, there are both wiser and more foolish ways to participate in this ministry of giving. As with all the other plays we have mentioned, generally speaking, the more direct and radical your giving, the more impact it will make!

We've already talked about how giving can fail to be radical enough. If you really believe that the part in the mission that God has for you to play is to financially support exported disciple makers, then why not get radical about it?

There are always voices in the church that encourage believers to make wise financial decisions based on biblical principles and to gradually build their personal wealth. Such advice is often useful for getting out of debt and learning to get control of the resources that God has given. But for the sake of the mission, it is vital that we recognize that our making wise financial decisions is not a means to create wealth, but a prerequisite for being radically involved in the Great Commission! It is not mission-focused to put a leash on your giving, hoping to someday be wealthy enough to give big money (without it hurting). If you want to play the position of "giver," then change the way you live and start giving as big as you can today! We are never commanded to plan our futures (which may not come!) so that we may be generous someday. We are to be generous now with however little we may have!

Now, let's talk about what increasing the directness of our giving looks like. If you are part of a denomination that supports missions through a cooperative program, think for a minute about how many hands your missions giving passes through before making an impact on the mission field. Though every hand between you and the field may belong to a man of integrity, there are still some drawbacks to this approach. For example, many of the churches that give through a denominational board in this way very rarely have any direct contact with missionaries on the field. This often tragically results in a general blindness to the world's condition and a blunted zeal for the mission. I'm far from against cooperative programs, but here's a suggestion: if this is your primary strategy for financial involvement in the Great Commission, you may want to supplement your giving by making a direct partnership with a particular missionary or two.

What do I mean by partnering with a missionary? I mean finding a missionary whom you have researched, contacted, visited and lifted up in prayer. I mean finding a missionary whose ministry excites you. Someone whose work is resulting in many *unheards* hearing the gospel. I mean directly moving money from your account to his on a regular basis. It may be someone whom you are already supporting through a cooperative program! So why do it? Because if you truly believe that "giver" is the position that God wants you to fulfill in His global mission, do you really want to be so passive with your investments? Mutual funds are great for people who don't want to think too much about what their money is doing, but career investors are out researching and buying shares they believe in! That's where the potential for real impact lies!

A Play for Pastors—Why Not Advocate?

I know I've already talked to churches as a whole, but I would still like to speak a brief aside to pastors for a moment. It would be hard to overstate your foundational role to the mission's accomplishment. You are the one who faithfully shepherds your congregation in their spiritual growth, guiding them into obedience to God's commands. As with any other matter of corporate obedience to God, pastors must make a continual effort to keep the command perpetually in front of their people. In other words, the pastor must become an advocate of the Great Commission. An advocate who reminds the people of their duty. An advocate who speaks on behalf of his Lord's command and glory. An advocate who represents millions of *unheards*.

One of my closest friends serves as a pastor in Georgia. Georgia the state, not the country (much to my chagrin). The two of us underwent missionary training together under my mentor in Peru. Though I'm the one who became a missionary, I can promise you that he has not taken his Great Commission responsibility even a bit less seriously. Instead, he has made an intentional decision to utilize his pastoral ministry to speak on behalf of specific places where there are many *unheards* and to cultivate laborers to go to those places. He has been rabidly pushing northern India for the past couple years. He has visited the region twice, he has searched high and low for missionaries working there, he has done extensive research on the area and he has tearfully pleaded in prayer and in preaching for laborers to go. As a result of his efforts over the space of a few years, a couple young families have decided to carry the gospel to that part of northern India. None of this has been part of his expected pastoral duties, but it has been part of his duties as an advocate!

Pastor, if you truly believe that you have already found your place in the plan and that you should not be exported to a place with a higher *unheard* factor, then why not make a radical decision to be an advocate for some unreached region? Your pastoral duties provide you with daily opportunities to confront believers in your flock with the needs of another place. Your preaching can be used to demonstrate to your congregation their biblical duty to proclaim the gospel to people in a place like Nepal. You can set aside special times in the church's calendar to highlight and pray for the need of a place like Malaysia. You can lead the church to make radical budget allowances to further the gospel in a place like Malawi. You can organize extraordinary trips that give members of your church firsthand exposure to a place like Papua New Guinea. You can also challenge the youth of your church to consider giving their lives as missionaries to a place like Saudi Arabia.

True, few of your members expect any of this from their pastor. But I would beg you not to forfeit the tremendous powers afforded you as a "remainer." As a pastor, you hold sway over far more resources than the average believer. Why not become an advocate for a particular place and ask God to multiply your Great Commission impact?

A Play for Educators—Why Not Streamline?

A friend of mine told me about his experience at his Bible college when he changed his major from pastoral studies to foreign missions. One week, not long after his switch, there was a special seminar for all of the pastoral students, featuring the president of the school and a visiting lecturer. Meanwhile, the missions majors were convened in the gymnasium for a goofy relay race featuring some stomach-turning foods! That was enough for my friend to figure out that the academic expectations of missionaries at his particular school were a bit of a joke.

That of course is an extreme case, but it reflects some commonplace thinking about the work of a missionary. Many Christians think the most important qualifications for a missionary are a strong stomach and a penchant for manual labor. These same peculiar ideas persist in the majority of institutions that claim to be preparing missionaries. In other words, when it comes to the process of training men and women for their future exportation, the playbook that many use is again insufficiently radical and direct.

In some schools, the training offered to missionaries is simply off target. Many, for example, embrace an outdated model of missionary training that concentrates on survival-type skills. Building construction, automobile repair and first aid are the kinds of courses that aspiring missionaries are asked to complete. What on earth for? Are we exporting a disciple maker or filming a Discovery Channel program? Suggesting skills like these as prerequisites for missionary service demonstrates a failure to appreciate the nature of the task at hand! Skills like these are useful in places where people are few; the Great Commission leads us most naturally to places where people are many!

The missionaries you are taking responsibility to train are going to be preaching the gospel to far more people who have never heard the gospel than those who will remain as pastors of Western churches! They need, then, all the skills that a Western pastor would need, and then some! Can they communicate God's Word persuasively to a society foreign to them? Can they effectively learn another language? Can they establish an indigenous church? Can they train well-rounded pastoral leadership in another culture? These are the skills that must be ingrained before exportation occurs. Honestly, if I were a prospective missionary enrolling in a school today, I would simply take whatever courses were suggested for church planters. The education provided in that track would be of much more use to a missionary than the content of most foreign missions tracks.

And then, many missionary training programs are just not radical enough. You could say that they're not streamlined to complete the training in as little time as possible. Educators, why not sit down with some veteran missionaries and figure out just what are the absolutely essential courses for an exported disciple maker? Why not make an option for students to pack all of those courses into as few years as possible? Let the students give up their summers and holidays, if they're willing! And why not think of ways to get them onto the mission field for a significant portion of their training? Students learn a great deal about the Christian life in a Bible college or seminary, but how many of them learn that a believer's time is of the essence?

When it comes to training missionaries, there are far more important considerations than diplomas, accreditation and the much-lauded college experience. Though my own training was far from orthodox, it was radical enough to prepare me for exported gospel ministry in ways that I don't believe a seminary would have. Why don't we start measuring our missionary training programs, not by the commonly-received academic standards, but by the urgency and momentousness of the mission?

A Play for Prospective Missionaries—Why Not Train?

Finally, a radical suggestion for prospective missionaries, for those who believe that their "X" should run forward with the gospel to places with many *unheards*. Why not train?

This is where so much missionary zeal crashes and burns. There is a real danger of oversimplification whenever we're talking about preparing for missionary service. When we endorse statements like, "We're really all missionaries already," or "Being a missionary just means sharing the gospel with others," we run the very serious risk that young men and women will charge out onto a raging battlefield without weapons or armor. While it's true that being a missionary is as simple as taking the gospel to those who don't have it, it is also true that there is always significant opposition to your doing so! There are innumerable ploys that will be used by the enemy to silence a gospel-proclaiming missionary.

I don't think this has ever been so clear to me as when I first arrived in northern China. Though we were prepared to be the only missionaries in town, we were surprised to find that we were far from alone! Tragically, we also found that the greater part of missionaries in China are ineffective as witnesses. Their preaching has been muted, either by a failure to learn the Chinese language, or by a schedule packed full of pre-Commission activities, or by an unhealthy fear of reprisals from the government, or by a lack of a strategy for planting churches or by one of a hundred other breakdowns. If you are a prospective missionary, those pitfalls should be sobering. Statistically, most missionaries will suffer the same fate!

I know of no prevention against these pitfalls that works half as well as a commitment to receive training from an experienced missionary. A strong and ongoing mentoring relationship with a veteran missionary (who has actually done what you hope to do) is a gracious means that God often utilizes to keep the missionary unentangled and moving toward the *unheards*. In our work in China, wise counsel has time and again meant the difference between the advance of the gospel and running pell-mell into a wall!

If you are persuaded that your missionary zeal should find expression in going as a missionary, I rejoice with you. May nothing deter you along the course you must run to bring the gospel to the lost. But I would implore you to realize that getting on an airplane and landing in a foreign field is not "mission accomplished" for a missionary. It is only the beginning of his work and his war. The untrained Christian is only slightly less likely to become ineffective in an unreached place as he was back home! Your role in the Great Commission is too vital to be wrecked for want of training. Why not go in the most radical way possible: in the footsteps of the men who have gone before you?

Radical Strategy

My hope has been simply that this chapter would get the gears turning in the strategic part of your mind. I know that there are some in the family of God who think the word "strategy" has no place in the believer's vocabulary, and I see what they mean. There have always been some in the church who have been deceived into believing that they could, by acting pragmatically, accomplish that which only the Holy Spirit can. I join you (I hope) in rejecting such an infringement on the freedom of God to do His own will. What we are talking about here is quite different, however. None of these suggestions to make direct and radical plays concern those actions that God has sovereignly reserved for Himself. Instead, they all concern our obedience to a mission that God has clearly appointed for us. When God's command comes to us, can we do any less than strive with all our energies to obey? That certainly includes striving with our powers of reason and calculation, deciding how we can most effectively perform the thing in which God delights. We expect to do no less for His other commands. Let's bring the same radical commitment to obey His Commission.

So what's your play? When the huddle breaks, do you know where you are going to run? I doubt many who would read a book like this have any intention of heading to the sidelines. Nonetheless, it behooves each of us to think about how hard we're running, and in what direction we're running. How radically committed are we to the mission? By God's grace, let us seek to pursue the lost with the same holy compassion with which He pursued us! His radical love makes reasonable service out of all our sacrifice!

13

A God Worth Proclaiming

How does our vision of God lead to our involvement in missions?

To wrap up this book, I want to talk about one more of my biblical missionary heroes. The account of his work is instructive for us in part because of its location in the Bible: in the heart of the Old Testament. I like that because it is very possible that as we near the end of our discussions about the Great Commission, there are still some readers who feel that such a relentless missionary focus is hopelessly reductionistic. They may wonder if we're not confusing a single element of our Christian mission with the whole of it. Maybe those who live with a disciple-making obsession will one day wake up and be embarrassed to discover that they were too focused on taking the gospel to the world. At this juncture of lingering doubts, I think we are served well by a look at the Old Testament.

The Essential Continuity of Missions

As we talked about way back in the beginning of this book, the centrality of world missions to our lives as God's people becomes apparent when we see the Great Commission as but the current dispensation of God's plan that has been in motion since creation. This is not necessarily to say that our current mandate to preach the gospel to the nations is either identical to or different from the mission given to believers before the New Covenant. Strong arguments have been given for both positions, but for our purposes here, it is only important to note that both positions depict an essential continuity between God's intentions now and then. That is, if we zoom out as far as revelation allows, what do we see God accomplishing in human history? From the creation of the world to its future recreation, we see God working all together for His own chosen good: the gracious redemption of a people for his own worship from among his enemies. This self-determination on God's part includes all His actions in the world leading up to the cross, and all of those that have been done among us as his people ever since.

So what does this continuity of God's plan mean for us? First of all, it means that our mission is not a secondary or remedial plan of God. We can take heart and rejoice in all of our disciple-making labors, knowing that they are all part of nothing less significant than God's cosmic will for mankind! Secondly, this continuity is also of great interest when we, standing in our particular moment of salvation history, reflect on the works of God recorded in the Old Testament. It means that we as Christians can, from the pages of the Old Testament, glean instruction, encouragement and direction regarding the mission left to us by our resurrected Lord.

Jesus spoke very clearly about the right way to understand the Old Testament: it was all about Him. He alone is the key to making sense out of what too often is perceived to be a grab-bag of history, law, prophecy and culture. From its first page to its last, the Old Testament forms a keyhole that can only be unlocked by the appearance of Christ. What this means for us as we consider the timelessness of our mission is that the work that Christ came to accomplish ultimately (the redemption of a people by His atonement) can also be seen in a more preliminary, seminal form in the pages of the Old Testament. This means that the mission that God has ordained for the church today is not totally disconnected from the commands given to God's people in Old Testament times. It means that wherever we find ourselves reading in Scripture, whether before or after the incarnation of the Son of God, we can expect to be instructed and challenged to fulfill our missional roles in God's original and uncompromised plan of redemption.

Thus, I personally have found that the Old Testament provides us with some of the most vivid illustrations of the work that we as New Testament missionaries are commissioned to do. When I read of the patriarchs and their wanderings, the children of Israel and their liberation or the divided kingdoms and their prophets, my own missionary zeal is oft replenished and reenergized. Again and again, we find the immutable plan of God conspicuously at work: a people is being redeemed from the sinful world to worship and glorify Him forever. Though the specific commands given to God's people at various points within salvation history do not bear a strong resemblance to our commission in this age, that essential continuity is still there. Seen in this light, the Old Testament bears its own treasury of missionary testimonies.

The Desecration of Baal's Altar

So without further ado, go back with me mentally to the period of the judges. These pages arguably represent the bleakest years of Israel's history. The once-glorious nation that bears the name of God now seems terribly like an infirm, senile old man. Repeatedly, the Israelites are plagued with an infection of idol worship, then ravaged by oppressors and brought to the threshold of extinction. Only in their final moments, from out of the throes of death, do they make a sudden, miraculous recovery and show the vitality of God's merciful power working within them; but it's not long before they are racked with yet another doxological ailment and drift towards death's door again (see Judg. 2:10-23).

In one of the deepest of those valleys of apostasy, where God's promises seemed to hang by a thread, the angel of the Lord appeared to Gideon, the son of a small-time clan ruler (see 6:11-12). The angel's message was simple: you will, by the power of the Lord's presence, deliver Israel from her oppressors (see 6:14). In Moses-like fashion, Gideon offers a protest that he is an unsuitable candidate for such a mission (see 6:15). But the angel assures Gideon that the Lord will work mightily through him (see 6:16). Then Gideon requests a sign, by which his eyes are opened to the terrifying reality of the Lord's presence (see 6:17-23). He builds an altar to the Lord who alone is the peace of His people (see 6:24).

All seems ready for the people to experience deliverance. The savior has been appointed. The enemy has been identified. The presence of the Lord has been promised. So the unsuspecting reader might be forgiven for expecting the battle with the Midianites to break out immediately. Of course, that reader would be mistaken. There are four intervening episodes whereby Gideon and the people are further prepared for war with the enemy: the destruction of Baal's altar (see 6:25-32), the dual testing with the fleece (see 6:36-40), the thinning of Israel's ranks (see 7:2-8) and the eavesdropping on the Midianite soldier's telling of his dream (see 7:9-15). Though all four episodes are unexpected, the first strikes me as strangest, for it seems to bear the least connection to the immediate crisis of starving Israelites and impending war with Midian.

This first episode occurs in the nighttime hours of the day that the angel appeared to Gideon. Gideon hears the voice of the Lord commanding him to desecrate his father's altar to Baal and the adjoining monument to Asherah (see Judg. 6:25-26). To ascertain the seriousness of this action, we need only to observe the strong emotions that surface in this story. Gideon doesn't carry out this task in the daytime because he is afraid of his father and the other men of the town (see 6:27)—and for good reason. For when the people find out what Gideon has done, they angrily call for his head (see 6:28-30)! This implies that this idolatry, while Gideon's father Joash may have been some kind of sponsor, had trickled down to the rest of the townspeople as well.

Gideon completes this "sacrilegious" vandalism by erecting an altar to the Lord in the place of the displaced altar to Baal and by offering his father's bull upon the wood of the broken-down monument to Asherah. The villagers wake up in the morning to discover that their beloved idols have been destroyed (see 6:28)! Instantly, a furious inquiry is made to root out the culprit. Soon the mob has their answer: Gideon son of Joash destroyed their image of Baal (see 6:29).

Now what could be the purpose of this mission? Just when Gideon is turning his thoughts to rallying the nation to join him in going to war with Midian, he is forced to turn his own clan against him! While we would all certainly agree that the presence of an idol is regrettable, the truly ominous threat seems to be centered in the Midianite army. Fighting them would seem to be job number one for an aspiring deliverer.

But the opening of Gideon's story makes the answer clear. The prophet sent from the Lord declares to the people of Israel that the oppression of the Midianites has been allowed by God to trouble them in response to their flouting His prohibition against worshiping the gods of the Canaanites (see Judg. 6:7-10). In other words, the Midianites are just a symptom of their weakened state, and not the cause itself. The real issue is that Israel has taken the worship that belongs to God alone and diverted it to false gods. So now, when God calls out His chosen deliverer, the first task He assigns him is to declare war on these false gods, not on the Midianites!

Still, this battle isn't over when the altar has been destroyed! The altar may lie in ruins, but the idol is still firmly planted in the hearts of this clan—and they want blood! They demand that Joash give his son into their hands for execution. Ironically, it is the words of Joash, the idol's proprietor, that serve to challenge the idol's place of honor in their town (see 6:31). Perhaps in his desperation to save his son's life, Joash begins to question Baal's very nature.

The logic of his response to the crowd's demands is simple: if Baal is a god, why does he need you to fight for him? If someone tore down his altar, why doesn't he rise up and do something about it (see 6:31)? His silence and inaction are proof positive that Baal is unworthy of your worship! Thus, a crushing blow is dealt to Baal's reputation. The god who contended with Jehovah could not even defend himself against the likes of pathetic Gideon! This revelation of an impotent Baal is exactly what God intended by His commission to Gideon. As if God were saying to Israel, "Look what you left me for! A god who can't defend himself!"

The weight of Gideon's actions was so great that they defined the way his people viewed him for the rest of his life! A new name was bestowed upon him: Jerubbaal, which means something like "Baal-fighter" (or, as I prefer, "what's-Baal-gonna-do-about-it?") (see Judg. 6:32). When the Israelites saw Gideon, they saw living proof of Baal's failure and frailty. Gideon's work marked a new era of freedom, not just from the oppression of Midian, but from the tyranny of Baal. Jerubbaal was the one who tore down the altar to Baal and brought back the altar to the Lord!

Declaring War on Idols

To appreciate the relevance of this episode to our modern missionary commission, it's essential that we keep our eyes trained on the horizons of biblical revelation. We must look through the lenses of God's continuous plan throughout human history. Again, what is God up to from beginning to end? He is redeeming a people for Himself. The real story behind human history is salvation history. Where does Gideon fit into this plan? The people God has chosen to worship Him are, in Gideon's time, in bondage to idol worship and its consequences. God's plan to redeem a people, then, involves His sending Gideon to liberate the Israelites from the gods they have chosen, that they may worship Him alone.

So in the commissioning of Gideon, we see some parallels to our own mission to preach the gospel. Gideon is sent to God's chosen people to demonstrate the evil and stupidity of preferring idols over the creator God. This is the real problem with which Gideon must contend as Israel's judge. We often think about the primary work of the judges in military terms, as they led Israel into legendary battles against their seemingly-invincible foes. But the office of judge was not merely occasional, as if judges were to be appointed only while there was a military threat to the nation of Israel. Instead, we are told repeatedly that a particular deliverer served as judge for many years in Israel. In the absence of Moses, Joshua or a king, the judges shouldered the responsibility of leading God's people to obey His covenant. As we saw above, Gideon had to declare war on Baal before it was time to go toe-to-toe with Midian.

There is a chronic tendency for Christians today, even missionaries, to confuse Midian and Baal. That is, there are countless heinous manifestations of sin's effects in our world today. It is a temptation to all ministers of the new covenant to go forth to war against those things, attempting to transform this fallen world into a land of peace and justice. But while sin's days are numbered, our current commissioning in the world sends us to fight, not with flesh and blood, but with the spiritual evil of idolatry. Our mission is a war with false worship, setting men and women free from slavery to their chosen gods.

We may very well rejoice when we see Midian's hold crippled. When we see the effects of sin in our family, society, workplace or government, we surely must mourn. But if we are truly burdened about sin's cancerous presence within our world, we would do well to heed our commission. For our exportation to the world with the message of Christ's gospel is the prescribed means whereby the masses of humanity enslaved to false gods may be finally and gloriously delivered.

In China, for instance, we find dozens of sin's malignant tumors eating away at the image of God as seen in Chinese culture and society. Corruption in the government, extreme economic injustice, the widespread and uninhibited practice of abortion and repression of religious liberties are just a few of the ills that will grieve the regenerated heart of a believer. Multiple times in our years in China, a new Christian has talked to us about how bothered they are by the political state of their country. Their new faith in Jesus has solidified in their minds what they perhaps already suspected: that they are living under a repressive government. You can almost see the wheels turning in their heads. Some of them will be bold enough to share their revolutionary sentiments out loud. While I sympathize, as there's little I would like more than a regime change in China, I have felt compelled in such cases to call these brothers and sisters back to the mission of the church. Change your world, by all means—but change it to one where Christ is king!

We as exported missionaries must remind ourselves constantly that none of those things are the real enemy. The true source of all these evils is to be found in the misdirected worship of individual men and women. The way to meaningfully participate in God's all-inclusive plan for human history in China is to strive to set those men and women free from their idols. We need the preaching of the gospel more than a solution for any of these problems. We need Jerubbaals before we need Jerubmidians.

Of course, there are not too many altars to Baal in China . . . or anywhere else for that matter. The Chinese people actually pride themselves on their history of being a nontheistic society. While that claim is itself demonstrably inaccurate, it is largely beside the point. Even if the Chinese had been godless, they would not be worshipless! No human ever has been. While many people in China and other nations may deny the existence of a creator, they are all hopelessly absorbed in the worship of His creation! They live to serve a vast pantheon of cruel deities.

So we as exported missionaries find ourselves in China as idol-destroyers. We proclaim the gospel to those who live and die for sex, wealth, fame, power and familial bliss. We seek to tear down the altars of the ideological false gods of materialism, humanism and Marxism. We are commissioned to liberate worshipers from false religion: from Buddhism, from Taoism and from atheism. Like Gideon before us, our works should stand as a testimony to the powerlessness of all these gods. We live in defiance of their whims, yet we are shielded from their capricious wrath! And we, like Paul, declare that men and women should turn from these vain gods to the God that created them.

What greater testimony could be given of our work as ministers of the new covenant than to be called a "Jerubbaal"? Imagine that you were to be exported as a missionary to Thailand, where 95 percent of the population call themselves Buddhists. Let's ignore for a second all of the other more subliminal idols that dictate the lives of sixty-five million Thai people. Imagine, then, that you spent the next thirty years of your life making disciples of Christ out of former Buddhists. Over the years, you saw worshiper after worshiper turn away from the altars of Theravada Buddhism to joyfully participate in the worship of the true Lord God of creation. When at last you complete your race on earth, can you imagine that some Thai disciples of Christ might joyfully call you a "Jerubbuddha"—one who lived a life of challenge to a false god? One who showed them that their god was a vain thing!

I pray that many of this generation will personally declare war on one of the myriad false gods holding millions of souls captive in some nation in this earth. May those Jerubbaals mobilize all their resources, cut themselves loose from all entanglements, and embrace all sacrifice in order to swing the mighty hammer of God's Word against the foundation of that idol's worship. This is the essence of our Great Commission: every disciple made for Christ is an altar of Baal cast down and a new temple of true worship to the Lord constructed in its place. O Lord, use our lives to do this, for Your great name's sake!

The True Jerubbaal

This examination of Gideon would be incomplete without a look at his ultimate failure. Of course, he did lead the Israelites to a miraculous victory over the Midianites, freeing the nation from their oppression. For forty years, the Israelites enjoyed peace under the judgeship of Gideon. But the war for God's worship had not yet reached its conclusion. Scripture tells us that as soon as Gideon was dead, the children of Israel again showed themselves unfaithful to God. They went after Baal again, restoring his idols to the place of prominence that Gideon had torn down. The Baal-fighter's victory was incomplete.

Anyone familiar with the remaining centuries of Old Testament history will know that the story of Baal was far from over. You probably remember the vivid accounts of Elijah's dramatic confrontation with hundreds of Baal's prophets at Mount Carmel. Maybe even the story of Jehu, the king of the northern kingdom, and how he called a great convocation of the prophets and worshipers of Baal. He lured in a houseful of idolaters, then sent in eighty armed men to slaughter them all! Yet, in spite of so many memorable and heroic battles against him, Baal would rear his head again and again! Not only was the original Jerubbaal's victory incomplete; the work of every other Baal-fighter that took up the mantle after him was also found wanting.

Baal didn't just barely cling to survival; he continued to deal major damage to Israel until finally, it was Baal who put Israel on the ropes. Israel's idolatrous ways eventually resulted in her captivity. Not just oppression from the likes of Midian, but decimation and slaughter at the hands of far more fearsome foes, Assyria and Babylon. The prophet Jeremiah showed this causal relation between the worship of Baal and the captivity of Israel most clearly (see Jer. 2:8; 7:9; 11:13, 17; 19:3-6; 23:13; 32:26-

35). He proclaimed that destruction and judgment were going to come upon the kingdom of Judah because the people, their kings and their prophets had repeatedly devoted themselves to idolatry. Baal's victory seemed well-nigh certain.

Now, if men like Gideon and Elijah can't exterminate idol worship from God's chosen people, how can we possibly expect to fare any better in our modern quest to win God's worship? If you launch out as a disciple maker to the ends of the earth, what hope can you have of delivering people from their bondage to their chosen gods? How can we expect any real, lasting good to come out of a mission to preach the gospel in China? If the idols ultimately overcame Jerubbaal's efforts, won't our own efforts suffer the same fate?

This is one of the last, but most significant, reasons that many believers will never dare to be exported. When they hear about the viselike hold that Islam has taken on the minds of men and women in Muslim countries, or when they hear about the hostility of certain governments toward the preaching of the gospel, there is a sense that all of our disciple-making efforts are doomed from the get-go! The idea that you could move to a remote city in northern India and make disciples may seem to belong to the same category as moving to Los Angeles and making it as a movie star. Incredibly unlikely, and only for those too foolhardy and simpleminded to know any better. The reasonable thing to do is to stay put.

Reasonable, that is, until you meet the supreme Jerubbaal!

If a few thousand years of human history had proved nothing else, they had certainly demonstrated beyond any doubt that man could not by his own efforts bring his fallen path back to God. He could not drive the car straight down the road, only swerve wildly from one ditch to the other, never making forward progress. God never would become his aim, his desire or his love. Gideon couldn't make them go straight. Elijah couldn't make them go straight. It is at this point that mankind could only look to God and say, "If you don't do it, it won't get done!"

And that's exactly what God intended to do! The Son humbled Himself to become a man. What was the Son of God doing living among a world of idolaters? He had come to destroy, like His forerunners in the Jerubbaal tradition. He had come to destroy the works not just of one false god, but of the father of stolen worship himself, the devil (see 1 John 3:8). He proclaimed that a new era of worship had arrived, in which God would become the true object of the affections and desires of those whom He had chosen out of the world. His people's hearts would no longer wander from their ultimate good, but would begin to move steadily toward Him.

How would Jesus Christ, God in human flesh, accomplish what the previous Baal-fighters could not? First, He lived a life that no other man, not even Gideon or Elijah, has ever lived: a life of unswerving worship toward the Father. A straight path without deviation. But then, second, He died the death of an idol-worshiper! The Israelite kingdoms had joined themselves to idols and had suffered national destruction and loss. Now Jesus hangs upon a cross, suffering all the pain, disjunction and disintegration that belongs to every one who endears himself to a false god.

What has all this death accomplished? In the destruction that He suffered, He paid the price for all of us idol-worshipers. He took the judgment that should righteously have been poured out on me as an idolater! The result, emphatically proven and actualized in the resurrection, is that God's chosen people can finally be fully delivered from the power of false gods! They will be freed by faith, in this work of the true Jerubbaal, to relate to God in the way He originally intended. Thus, God's panoramic plan for human history is achieved: a people is graciously redeemed, out from among the mass of fallen humanity, who will worship Him forever.

Remember what it was that alerted Joash to the untenability of idol worship? It was His realization that Baal was a god who could not fight for himself. By inference, the true God would be well able to undertake his own self-defense! He would be able to fight for his own worship. This is exactly what we see in the gospel! The gospel is the message that God has fought for Himself, defending His own glory from the false gods vaunted by mankind.

I'm happy to end this book here because this is something that every disciple-making missionary must know. It is perfectly incomprehensible to the world that you should attempt to pro-actively seek out people of one faith and convert them to an-other, i.e., make them disciples of Christ. And they will ask you why! "We already have our own beliefs. Why would you want to change them?" A missionary must know a hundred ways to answer that question, and they must be well-worn, hard-hitting, crystal clear answers if our preaching is to have any persuasive-ness at all!

Gideon shows us one of those wonderfully clear answers. Ev-ery other religion in the world tells you to fight on God's behalf. The outcome of the epic battle between good and evil relies on the efforts of the faithful. If a Muslim or a Buddhist or a Hindu or an animist wishes to make himself one of God's people, he must work as hard as he can to overcome his own bent toward sin. The Lord is unique among the idols of the world in that He fights His own battle and, what's more, that He fights our battle for us! We are not victorious for Him; we are victorious in Him. The message, then, that we are preaching to the world as missionaries is not that they must fight for their salvation, but that the true Jerubbaal has already done all that is necessary for them to be liberated from sin's clutches.

This answer in turn becomes a powerful motivator for missionaries. When I see that He fought (to the death) for me so that the cell of my own idolatry would be unlocked, I suddenly have the capacity to love others enough to fight for their freedom! I can give my life to go preach the gospel to people who are now strangers to me.

Finally, this answer becomes the missionary's confidence. What hope does a disciple maker have in China or Morocco? None without the cross. Without the cross, I could have no freedom from sin myself, let alone think about delivering glorious life to a Chinese person. With the cross, I experience firsthand, unprecedented liberation to true worship, and I know therefore that if this freedom could be mine, it might also be Wei Tao's, or Liu Miao's, or Xu Ning's or Tian Yi's! My disciple-making efforts no longer seem doomed—the prospects now seem bright! It is He who fights for us in northern China—and that's what makes it reasonable that we should go—or that you should go.

That's all this book has been about. I have tried to show the eminent reasonableness of becoming an exported disciple maker. A thousand factors might portray missions as an indefensible endeavor, but the cross of Christ overrides them all! It dwarfs in importance all of our interests, our ambitions, our misgivings, our preferences and our plans. When we see the cross of Christ, nothing is more reasonable than to rush with joyful hearts to the world, proclaiming the victory that He won on our behalf!

Notes

1. Rodney Stark, *What Americans Believe* (Waco: Baylor Press, 2008).

2. Ed Stetzer, "Dropouts and Disciples: How Many Students Are Really Leaving the Church?," *Christianity Today*, May 14, 2014, http://www.christianitytoday.com/edstetzer/2014/may/dropouts-and-disciples-how-many-students-are-really-leaving.html.

3. David Crabb, "Bruce Ware Interview, Contemporary Issues," davecrabb.com, April 2, 2012, http://www.davecrabb.com/2012/04/03/bruce-ware-interview/.

4. Kevin DeYoung, "Spirit-Powered, Gospel-Driven, Faith-Fueled Effort,"2012 T4G Conference, July 24, 2014, https://www.youtube.com/watch?v=AlkQP1KWAnI.

5. William Carey, *An Enquiry into the Obligations of Christians to Use Means in the Conversion of the Heathens*, (Leicester: 1792).

6. Wayne A. Grudem, *Making Sense of the Church: One of Seven Parts from Grudem's Systematic Theology*, new ed., (Grand Rapids: Zondervan, 2009).

7. Ruth A. Tucker, *From Jerusalem to Irian Jaya: A Biographical History of Christian Missions*, 2nd ed. (Grand Rapids: Zondervan, 2011).

8.   Ibid.

9.   Ibid.

10.   Justo Gonzalez, *The Story of Christianity*, vol. 1, 2nd ed. (New York: HarperOne, 2014).

11.   Rodney Stark, *The Rise of Christianity* (San Francisco: Harper, 1997).

12.   Bruce L. Shelley, *Church History in Plain Language*, 2nd ed. (Nashville: Thomas Nelson, 1996).

13.   Erroll Hulse, "John Calvin and his Missionary Enterprise: Missionaries Sent into France," *Reformation Today*, 1998, http://reformed-theology.org/html/issue04/calvin.htm.

14.   Timothy George, *Faithful Witness: The Life and Mission of William Carey* (Birmingham: New Hope, 1991).

15.   Carey, *An Enquiry into the Obligations of Christians to Use Means in the Conversion of the Heathens.*

16.   Daniel B. Wallace, "The Great Commission or the Great Suggestion," danielwallace.com, February 17, 2014, http://danielbwallace.com/2014/02/17/the-great-commission-or-the-great-suggestion/.

17.   Count Nicolaus Ludwig von Zinzendorf quotation in Missions and Evangelism quotes, accessed on December 1, 2014, http://www.tentmaker.org/Quotes/evangelismquotes.htm.

18.   Patrick Johnstone, *The Future of the Global Church* (Colorado Springs: InterVarsity Press/Authentic Media/GMI, 2011).

19. James Paton, *The Story of John G. Paton, or Thirty Years Among South Sea Cannibals* (New York: A.L Burt Co., 1890).

20. John Piper, *Filling up the Afflictions of Christ: The Cost of Bringing the Gospel to the Nations in the Lives of William Tyndale, Adoniram Judson, and John Paton*, The Swans Are Not Silent Series vol.5 (Wheaton: Crossway Books 2009).

21. Grudem, *Making Sense of the Church: One of Seven Parts from Grudem's Systematic Theology*.

22. George, *Faithful Witness: The Life and Mission of William Carey*.

23. John Piper, *Let the Nations Be Glad*, 2nd ed. (Ada: Baker Academic, 2003).

24. Stark, *The Rise of Christianity*.

PUBLICATIONS
Fort Washington, PA 19034

This book is published by CLC Publications, an outreach of CLC Ministries International. The purpose of CLC is to make evangelical Christian literature available to all nations so that people may come to faith and maturity in the Lord Jesus Christ. We hope this book has been life changing and has enriched your walk with God through the work of the Holy Spirit. If you would like to know more about CLC, we invite you to visit our website:
www.clcusa.org

To know more about the remarkable story of the founding of CLC International we encourage you to read

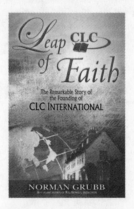

LEAP OF FAITH

Norman Grubb

Paperback
Size 5¹/₄ x 8, Pages 248
ISBN: 978-0-87508-650-7
ISBN (*e-book*): 978-1-61958-055-8